WHY THEY DIE

Curing the Death Wish in Our Kids

DR. JERRY JOHNSTON
with DON SIMMONDS

Foreword by Jay Lowder

crossroads

Praise for *Why They Die*

"Dr. Jerry Johnston has listened to and spoken in person to more teenagers than any other person I know. Over the past 25 years, he has become a recognized authority in helping mend broken lives. Following his studies at Acadia University in Nova Scotia, Canada, he earned a doctorate. He was assigned for his thesis a research subject with 15 words in the title. I asked him to summarize his research in simple language. This was it— "Why some clergy crash and burn out." Now in this book, Dr. Johnston has returned to his first love in ministry, our youth. He has focused his research, his vast experience, his excellent mind and his great heart on the reasons for what appears to be an epidemic of suicidal tendencies and acts of self destruction. Thanks, Dr. Jerry Johnston, for caring for our kids."

David Mainse
Founder, Crossroads Christian Communications

"Bewildered, families wander about, confused, in a daze, trying to piece together reasons why their son or daughter, brother or sister took their life. Leaving a gap for a lifetime, this life-ending moment seems to have little to no solution. Jerry Johnston in Why They Die opens this conversation in a way that leads to awareness and prevention. Read this book for all its worth, then pass it on. Shine light on this topic of darkness so others will not walk in its shadows."

Dr. Brian C. Stiller
Global Ambassador, the World Evangelical Alliance

"Jerry Johnston has spoken to more than 4,000,000 teenagers in high school assemblies across this continent. He has spoken one-on-one to thousands and has received letters and phone calls from thousands more. He has listened to the sobs of a fourteen-year-old girl who has had an abortion and wants to kill herself. He has listened to the anger of a sixteen-year-old boy who lies paralyzed from a drunk-driving accident."

Dr. Josh McDowell

"Jerry Johnston has his heart on the pulse of today's teens like few others. You will be deeply moved and informed by the biblical answers he provides for the 21st century problems our anti-Christian culture forces young people to cope with."

Dr. Tim LaHaye

"Dr. Jerry Johnston has provided an excellent resource that will benefit anyone who loves young people. Whether you are a parent, grandparent, or youth leader, this book will help you better understand the teenage suicide crisis in our culture and equip you to help youth in your circle of influence."

Dr. Bruce Fawcett
President/Vice Chancellor, Crandall University

"Anyone who has done hands-on youth work will immediately realize that Jerry Johnston has been listening."

Dr. Jay Kesler
Former President of Youth for Christ

"Happily married to his beautiful wife Cristie Jo and the father of three happy, healthy children, Jerry clearly understands his own stake in the youth of America. He serves as the spiritual

leader, example, and mentor to his own children; but he also knows that many kids do not have the benefit of a loving home with parents who truly care for them. To many of these kids Jerry has become the father figure, the older brother, and the inspirational example that many of them so desperately need."

Dr. Zig Ziglar

"In today's post-Christian age many people have lost their way. We have become a society that is biblically illiterate, theologically ignorant, and morally apathetic. It is not surprising that many ills are now epidemic, among them suicide. Dr. Jerry Johnston's new book, 'Why They Die,' speaks directly and effectively to this serious problem. This is a book that Christians must read. It is a book that we must share with family and friends and with anyone we care about."

Dr. Craig Evans
Acadia University Divinity College

"Dr. Jerry Johnston's new book, 'Why They Die: Curing the Death Wish in Our Kids' is disturbing, inspiring, and written with both the sensitivity of a father and the authority of a prophet. A man who has dedicated his life to ministering to youth, Johnston writes with both the insights of one who has 'been there done that' and the concerns we all have at what Maclean's magazine calls 'The Broken Generation.' What I truly appreciate about his work is that he 'lights a candle' rather than merely 'cursing the darkness.' Once you've read the book you'll have a sense of who and what today's youth are, and the difficult path they walk in the 21st century."

Jim Cantelon
Host of *100 Huntley Street*

WHY THEY DIE: Curing The Death Wish In Our Kids

Dr. Jerry Johnston with Don Simmonds

Published by Crossroads Christian Communications Inc.
1295 North Service Road
P.O. Box 5100
Burlington, ON L7R 4M2
www.crossroads.ca

Cover & Interior Design: Laura MacDermid
Editors: Danny Zacharias, Nancy Reed
ISBN: 978-1-896930-50-3

Printed in Canada

ALSO BY DR. JERRY JOHNSTON

Who's Listening:
What Our Kids Are Trying To Tell Us

Inspire Your Kids To Greatness

It's Killing Our Kids: Teenage Alcohol Abuse
and Addiction

The Last Days of Planet Earth

How To Save Your Kids From Ruin

The Edge of Evil

Why Suicide? What Parents and Teachers
Must Know to Save Our Kids

Going All The Way:
The Real World of Teens and Sex

Similarities and Differences
of Belief Systems

Daniel: Principles of Leadership,
Success, and Achievement

The Thrilling Prophesies of Mr. Z and Jesus

Crossroads Christian Communications Inc.

Crossroads Chairman and CEO, Don Simmonds, celebrated the 50-year anniversary of this fruitful ministry with founders, David and Norma Jean Mainse, at a recent historic Gala with ministry friends and supporters. *100 Huntley Street*, the flagship television program of Crossroads, began on June 15, 1977 and is the longest running daily Christian television program in Canada. Crossroads provides relevant messages of faith and inspiration for millions of Canadians and people around the world. Crossroads interacts with its viewers via 24/7 prayer lines, and has also been a highly respected and effective not-for-profit aid agency for over 25 years, having responded in times of natural disaster worldwide, raising funds and partnering with on-site, non-government organizations for emergency relief and long-term rebuilding strategies.

Don Simmonds leads the exciting vision for the future through a dramatic expansion of Crossroads outreach that reaches all ages at all stages with an effective increase of media programs and content that is harnessing all media platforms. The *Crossroads TV* project is a multiple-channel Internet platform, connecting to nearly four billion people globally and creatively proclaiming faith and values. As an extension of their mission, *Crossroads USA* was launched to touch all of North America for Jesus Christ.

The Crossroads Centre Prayer Lines, **1-866-273-4444**, (available in Canada and the United States) are available 24/7 to minister to you and help you follow Jesus Christ. Visit the ministry web site at **www.crossroads.ca.** Peruse the Crossroads **estore** to obtain excellent resources to build your faith. Go to **www.100huntley.com** for all online video resources and search by topic, guest, or date. Be sure to email

with your questions or prayer requests to
ministry@crossroads.ca.

Your financial support is essential for Crossroads to continue
its long tradition of faithfully proclaiming the Good News
of Jesus Christ. Mail your tax-deductible contribution to:
**Crossroads, P. O. Box 5100, 1295 North Service Road,
Burlington, Ontario L7R 4M2** or in the **United States** at:
Crossroads USA, P. O. Box 486, Niagara Falls, NY 14302 or
you can give online at www.crossroads.ca.

When you are in the Burlington area, stop by for a visit at
the Crossroads Centre for individual prayer or a tour of our
studios at 1295 North Service Road, Burlington, Ontario,
Canada; 905-332-6400.

Crossroads considers it an honour to serve and strengthen
you in your walk with God.

Contents

Acknowledgements

Mark Twain once wrote, *"Ideally a book would have no order to it, and the reader would have to discover his own."* The origin and order of this book deserves a great deal of gratitude.

Don and Fay Simmonds—thank you for your tireless efforts for young people for so many years. You both epitomize how much a couple can do who truly care. Don, thank you for your challenging vision for Crossroads coupled with such a passionate, caring heart.

Gary Gerard, thank you for your wisdom on behalf of the supporters and friends of Crossroads, and being so sensitive to find just the right resources to build their faith and evangelistic fervor. You are a faithful and good brother.

Cristie Jo and Jenilee, thank you for the many hours of reviewing the manuscript and making so many helpful suggestions. Cristie Jo, you are my best friend and soul mate!

Laura MacDermid, exceptionally talented Creative Lead at Crossroads, thank you for going the extra mile and shaping this book to be a resource, help, and guide to youth and parents everywhere.

Rick and Karla Moore, two of my dearest friends, who have stood so close to Cristie and me. Endless thanks. Karla combed through the manuscript and provided helpful ideas and corrections.

Danny Zacharias, lecturer in Biblical studies and technology assistant, at my alma mater, Acadia University Divinity College, for proofing the manuscript.

David Mainse, a man whose life is distinguished by such abundant spiritual fruit. Thank you for caring for lost, meandering people and having the vision to establish a Prayer Centre Hotline, 1-866-273-4444 so many years ago. Thank you for your compassion, and your tears for men and women who need Christ.

Dedication

To my loving God who saved me from taking my own life.

To a caring Dad who received my crisis call
and rushed home in time.

To all the people in the world searching for hope.

Foreword

Long-term exposure to darkness can decrease the ability of the eye to process light. So it is with the heart and soul. There is a place so hopeless, so deceivingly inescapable that people are driven to make an irrevocable decision to exterminate their own life. This pinnacle of self-crisis is the precise capsule I found myself entrapped in as a 21-year-old man.

I was raised in a healthy environment with excellent parents who provided all the building blocks for a successful and meaningful life. My father was a prominent businessman while my mother stayed home to raise my two sisters and me. Our family was anchored and traditional. My drift into the waters of self-violence was inconceivable. After moving off to attend college, I finished my first semester on academic probation and returned home. Eventually, I moved in with an old friend from high school and dove deeper into self-denial and depression. A smorgasbord of bad decisions, alcohol abuse, the ending of a key relationship and the loss of my job and car triggered ideas of me having nothing to live for. With each passing day my thoughts of suicide became more saturating. My inability to deal with a lack of hope reached a boiling point as I awakened with a severe hangover on a sunny spring afternoon. Stumbling into the bathroom, I lowered my face toward the sink and began splashing my face with cool water in an attempt to extinguish the burning fire on my forehead. When I raised my head and looked in the mirror, I began to scream at my own reflection, "I hate you! I hate you! I hate you!" I wanted to escape the person I had become as well as the tortuous pain I felt. At that moment, I decided to end my life. Sitting on the sofa in a trashed out duplex, I reached underneath the cushions and gripped my 22-caliber pistol. With my face drenched in tears, my hands shaking, and my entire body trembling in fear, I pointed the gun barrel at my temple. As I pressed the trigger, I heard someone pull onto our gravel driveway. It was my roommate. He came home from work early because his employer told him to take the rest of the day off as a reward for his hard work. Could it be coincidence or was God somehow trying to stop me from ending it all? I wasn't sure of the answer but the question plagued me enough to put a halt on the plan.

Weeks later I stopped by my parents' house to wash clothes and heard my mom hollering my name from the den. She had previously seen a commercial featuring a young charismatic speaker named Jerry Johnston. He was going to be speaking at an upcoming event and she was calling out because she wanted me to see the advertisement and to consider going to hear him. Ironically, she had no idea I was on a mental see- saw debating whether or not to end my life. When I walked in the room she just pointed to the TV. I caught just enough to hear him say he had attempted suicide. Although it was brief, when I heard him talk I felt riveted and unexplainably drawn to his every word. I knew he identified with my struggle and the treacherous path I was walking. Several weeks later his event began and I snuck in the balcony of the auditorium to hear what he was offering. For thirty minutes I was held captive by every sentence he uttered. Jerry explained he had found hope and direction through a genuine, life altering faith in God. By the end of his message, dozens of people, including myself, responded to an invitation to a new way of life. It was the turning point that brought clarity to a very dark existence.

After seeing and hearing how Jerry used the adversity from his past as a platform to reach out and help others, I became inspired to do the same. I couldn't have been a more unlikely candidate considering I was fresh off the skid of a suicide attempt, but that didn't change my determination to point others toward hope and salvation. Slowly, but surely, doors began to open for me to be a conduit to aid others. In the years since, I have been honored to address NFL football teams, churches, businesses, and an innumerable number of students on high school and college campuses. My story has been chronicled on national television, radio and in my first published book. These privileges were sparked the night I found faith through the message of Jerry Johnston.

This book is a lighthouse for anyone sinking in the depths of hopelessness. Jerry doesn't mimic words he has heard others speak. Simply put, he has been there. He is no stranger to pain, hopelessness and despair. He uses those experiences to direct others toward a life of freedom. His passion and scope of influence on the hurting and hopeless speaks for itself. Countless numbers of people have experienced faith, forgiveness, and a meaningful future through his talks, lectures, and books. His communication skills through the spoken and written Word are unparalleled. If you or someone you know struggles with suicidal tendencies, this book will be a great compass of direction.

A famous NFL football coach was once asked this question about a legendary running back. "Is he in a class all by himself?" The coach responded, "If he's not, it's a pretty small class." The same can be said of Jerry regarding his knowledge of suicide and his ability to speak to those in its grasp. I pray you find the light and peace I found in the following pages.

Jay Lowder
President of Jay Lowder Harvest Ministries Inc.
Author of *"Midnight In Aisle 7"* (Charisma House Publishers)
www.jaylowder.com

"Jay has spoken in over 350 crusades, rallies, and conferences. He has been invited to speak to numerous groups including NFL teams. He has been interviewed on ABC, The Discovery Channel, Fox, and profiled in SBC Life, Charisma, and ESPN Outdoors. God has given Jay a very special gift to reach people for Christ and I recommend him to pastors everywhere." **- Dr. Jerry Johnston**

Introduction

Don Simmonds, Chairman and CEO of Crossroads Christian Communications Inc.

A "perfect storm" is a rare combination of circumstances resulting in an event of unusual magnitude. You may remember the movie *The Perfect Storm*, where an unusually intense storm pattern caught some commercial fishermen unaware, putting them in mortal danger. That storm was created from a collision between a high-pressure system, a low-pressure system and the remnants from a dying hurricane.

Like the perfect storm, the youth of North America are caught unaware, in multiple cultural storms that converge into a force so formidable and so devastating, that our young people, with so much to offer, can get caught and are not able to get out.

Your own kids, like most of the youth in North America and around the world, face these converging, perilous storms:

- The Storm of Diluted Values

- The Storm of Failing Faith Foundations

- The Storm of Media Dominance

- The Storm of Personalizing Technology

In chapter four, I will tell you Dylan's touching story. Dylan was one of my young hockey players who took his life due to these devastating storms.

The Storm of Diluted Values

Take a look at what people consider being morally acceptable within our society today *(illustration on next page)*.

Moral Issue	2010
Divorce	69%
Gambling	61%
Sex Between Unmarried Men and Women	59%
Having a Baby Outside of Marriage	54%
Gay/Lesbian Relations	52%
Abortion	38%
Suicide	15%

Gallup's Annual Values and Beliefs Survey 2010

Decaying values permeate almost all areas of relationships. Self-focus is rampant. Bullying is an epidemic. Seventy-nine percent of respondents surveyed feel people are ruder to each other now than just ten years ago.

If we had clear measurements over time of how we are doing as a culture regarding morality, respect, fulfillment, or relationships, all would be on a dramatic trend line downward because the strength of our values has been diluted.

The Storm of Failing Faith Foundations

We can virtually forecast the social fabric of the future by studying what youth and young adults are thinking today because it won't be long before our youth will lead in our land. Lately, much has been done to capture the views of those aged 18-34, giving us an idea of what the future holds. Look at the comparison reflected in the following graph.

The survey asks the question: *Which of the following have you done in the last week? (graph on next page)*

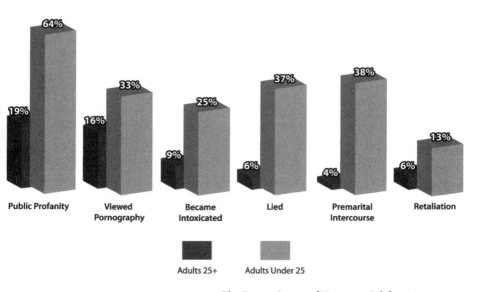

Public Profanity · Viewed Pornography · Became Intoxicated · Lied · Premarital Intercourse · Retaliation

Adults 25+   Adults Under 25

The Barna Group of Ventura, California
(www.barna.org) research 2008

With dark grey showing adults over 25, and light grey showing young adults between the ages of 18-25, we find that younger people use profanity three times as much, view pornography twice as much, get drunk three times as much, lie six times as much, have sex outside of marriage nine times as much and retaliate twice as much.

I have coached hockey in our community for some 20 years and currently have the privilege to be the head coach of the Uxbridge Tigers, our community's high school varsity hockey team. Our motto is "Winning at hockey and winning in life" so we work hard to model and teach character and broaden what it means to be a whole hockey player; not just hockey skills, but also intellectual development, physical well-being, relationships, and inner self.

Several years ago, I thought it would be a good idea for every player to sign a contract clearly setting out their commitment to not smoke, drink or take drugs; to respect those in authority over them (their parents, teachers, coaches and team captains) to make sure their schoolwork took priority over their hockey, and to agree to always put the overall team's interests above their own.

You can imagine how disappointed I was when I received a call from the school one day saying one of my players was suspended from school for three days for "smoking up" (drug use) on the bus. This young man never played another game with the Tigers, because he had made a clear commitment and he failed to live up to it so I had to follow through with the agreed upon consequences and remove him from the team. But, in a team meeting soon after the incident, I asked the rest of the team if they knew why he had been taken off the team, and with no hesitation, one young man said, "because he agreed not to get *caught* smoking up."

This view of this commitment showed me just how far the integrity reference among our youth had moved.

Recently, I was with a number of senior youth leaders reflecting together on new study on Canadian youth entitled "*Hemorrhaging Faith*." The study revealed that of youth growing up in our churches, and having already expressed a personal belief in God, only 23 percent (about 1 in 4) would describe themselves as still committed to God once they hit their young adult years. Many of those young people are abandoning faith and turning toward atheism (the belief that there is no God). With that decision their moral compass dissolves.

So we can see the Storm of Failing Faith Foundations is quickly advancing. You may have a son or daughter, or grandchild that you are concerned about and don't need any statistics to prove this storm is real.

Growing up with Christian parents, Dylan, was in a standoff with his mom and dad in grade ten. His parents gave him a clear ultimatum that they would not condone his having sexual relations with his girlfriend in their home. So Dylan decided to leave. What happened? His girlfriend's parents welcomed him to their place!

We have created a culture whose god is "freedom".

But when one's freedom becomes their god, truth, as a plumb line for life, is discarded. We make fun of accountability, we worship tolerance, entitlement is aroused (known as narcissism; the belief that the world revolves around us) and of course, instead of the logic of consistency keeping us on track, we simply conclude that contradictions are acceptable. All of this gives way for a person to question the very existence of God Himself.

While the Storm of Diluting Values has been at work, along comes the Storm of Failing Faith Foundations, excusing the need to follow the instructions for living that our Creator had in mind. But there is yet another storm...

The Storm of Media Dominance

This storm has been rising for some time now. There are two concerns regarding the storm of media dominance; the *content* and the *volume* of media consumed. In 2010, weekly online Internet usage increased more than the number of hours spent watching television. But, the number of hours watching television also increased, creating an absolute dominance of media in our lives! Studies reveal that the messages and volume of media consumed, accounts for behavioral issues in society. These issues include poorer grades, unrealistic viewpoints, instilling unnecessary fear and desensitizing and conditioning people in all kinds of ways.

Accompanied by music and magazines, the amount of media consumption, especially by the young, is nothing short of alarming. By the time a young person is age 17, they have consumed 63,000 hours of media compared to 11,000 hours in school, 2,000 hours in meaningful conversation with their parents, and just 800 hours in church. The media is distorting the world God has intended for us. The media does it by presenting these distortions, as facts, for an unsuspecting young generation. It is doing so in such loud volume and in such high stimulation, that young people almost don't have a chance!

Back in 1990, Dr. James Dobson in his book, *Children at Risk*, issued a clear warning about this. He put it this way:

> *Nothing short of a great Civil War of values rages today throughout North America. Two sides with vastly differing and incompatible world views are locked in bitter conflict that permeates every level of society...Children are the prize to the winners... those who control what young people are taught and what they experience—what they see, hear, think, and believe—will determine the future course for the nation.*[a]

So, who is winning?

There are some people who simply refuse to believe that behaviors are so adversely affected by the media. Recently, I listened to the news the morning after a jury convicted Michael Rafferty for the kidnapping, brutal rape, and first degree murder of little eight-year-old Tori Stafford. This was an event that held her family, the town of Woodstock, and indeed, the whole nation in a certain grip over the past few years.

Through a technicality, a judge would not let the jury see evidence that Michael Rafferty had an obsession with pornography about child rape and not long before the tragic incident, he had watched movies about the kidnapping and murder of little girls. His online name was "Mychol," and for years he trawled the lowest depths of the Internet, looking for images of child rape and torture. If you read the detailed account of the media Michael Rafferty consumed within 10 days of committing such a brutal crime, you would not wonder about this "media affect" anymore. Who is winning? It is a frightful reality… this Storm of Media Dominance.

The Storm of Personalizing Technology

If these three storms are not enough, there is one more storm system just coming into view now. With my background being from the technology industry, technology advances are not normally startling for me. But the last two or three years of technology advancement have ushered in quite a new and unique storm, which is adding a dangerous magnifying effect. It is the personalization of the full power of the new technologies that presents the concern. In the past, we would gather around a television set, or listen to the stereo speakers or radio together. But now, all of the powerful influences we have considered here are delivered directly, in high definition quality and sound, to the ears and eyes of our young people. A parent cannot hear what is on the TV in the other room and say, "I asked you not to watch that, please turn it off." Pornography is free flowing, and as mobile and personal as a cellphone or iPad.

Photographs, private texts, games, movies, and applications of all kinds are accessible to and shared among young people with virtually all of the same power that used to be at home under the accountability and surveillance of parents, siblings, and caregivers. In the hours that followed the horrific experience of Dylan's death, his dad, Jamie, was finally able to truly understand his son. It was made known through a review of the hidden electronic world in which Dylan lived. Technology had so personalized relationships, communications, music, photos, movies and other media consumption, that only then could Jamie finally see the traumatic nature of a life that was pulled and tugged into two different worlds. One world with hope and light where Dylan interacted with them and others with a positive influence in the world that God had intended; and a second dark, profane and hidden world of lies that tugged at him personally and privately.

God had given us a storm warning already in his Word. It

is found in Romans 12:2:

> *"Do not conform to the pattern of this world, but be transformed by the renewing of your mind. Then you will be able to test and approve what God's will is—his good, pleasing and perfect will." NIV*

This final storm system of personalizing technology allows such a powerful and direct saturation of the mind, that, added to the other storms that have been brewing already, creates a perfect storm that will affect our children and grandchildren in a proportion never before experienced by the human race.

For the last 35 years, I've been a Christian businessman, father, coach and ministry leader—the whole time this perfect storm has been brewing. Even as I summarize this situation for us, I have to admit to myself and to you—that this perfect storm has happened on *my watch!*

During this same period we have strived to meet the incredible needs of human suffering around the world in marvelous ways. We have found ways to alleviate hunger, and thirst, and improve the challenge of diseases like Aids in far-away places. All the while, right under our feet, right on our own doorsteps, we have allowed a culture that is so physically cared for and materially wealthy, to become spiritually bankrupt.

And it has happened on my watch... and yours!

It is time all of us found a way to head straight into this perfect storm armed with God's power and purpose. As the Chairman and CEO of Crossroads, I pledge to lead our team, with your support, to creatively and aggressively use the media to teach faith and values to *all ages* at *all stages* in life. We intend to counter this storm raging for the minds of our youth. Your partnership with us is essential. Thank you for your confidence in us. The job before us is mammoth but little is much when God is in it. We will be a careful steward of your support and, by using the same media power, will reach as many young people and families possible with the Good News of Jesus Christ.

CHAPTER 1

"Dad, I'm Going to Kill Myself."

*"Jerry, we'll do something. Son, please hold on.
What can I do?"*

People often ask me why I am so passionate about helping both youth and adults who exhibit suicidal tendencies. My own story will help you understand the profound compassion I have for people who are filled with utter despair and many of them who are seriously contemplating suicide. Everyone has a story to tell and by honestly sharing life's most challenging experiences and how they are overcome, we immediately connect with and help those who struggle. I have never concealed how utterly confused and lost I was as a teenager, nor how dire my outlook on life truly was. I believe transparency and vulnerability are the connection points in allowing me to bond with millions of kids worldwide who sit riveted while instantaneously identifying with similar issues.

At fourteen, alone and miserable, I laid at one end of the sofa in our family room feeling like the dark paneled walls were caving in on me. My parents and four brothers were away at work and school. All of them totally unaware of the tormenting battle raging within me. In my limp and lethargic state, I laid there for the longest time, almost catatonic, with my eyes intensely focused on the telephone in the distance near the kitchen. I believed it to be the final means of contact for help before ending my life. I felt nauseatingly sick and confused. I was convinced there was no way out of the misery I suffered. Weary from enduring months of physical and emotional torment as a result of excessive partying, drug use, and rebellion toward adult authorities in my life, I sensed an eerie and uncontrollable force compelling me to take that final destructive turn down a dead end street and end it all. At that point, the only thing that seemed to make any sense was death. My emotions were unstable and my mind transported me toward a vantage point where I could see myself lying in a coffin, peaceful and finally at rest. This seemed to be a logical consequence and fitting conclusion to my failed attempt at life.

I lay there on the sofa, tightly wrapped in my dad's big light blue bathrobe. From the time I came home from one of my first hospital stays, I wore that ugly, oversized robe. It wasn't so much that I was physically cold, but instead it was an indirect gesture for help or perhaps my feeble attempt to feel closer to my father, because we certainly could not communicate. Before my two hospitalizations, suspicion, mistrust, and arguments marred our relationship and created an icy condition between the two of us. Whenever dad disciplined me, and that was often, I would threaten to turn him in to the authorities for child abuse. But the onset of my physical problems soon changed that warlike environment. Eventually, instead of screaming at me, my parents consoled me, insisting, "Everything is all right, everything is going to get better." Sadly, things did not get better. I became more withdrawn, even docile.

With Mom and Dad both at work and my four brothers at school, my thoughts were running wild. The antique clock on the mantel ticked with an eerie rhythm that synchronized with my bizarre, almost overwhelming thoughts of taking my life. My eyes slowly shifted from focusing on the telephone toward the television where my mother had neatly displayed individual family pictures in decorative frames. Something compelled me and I managed to raise my listless body from the sofa and sluggishly pace over to the television. One by one I picked up each picture and studied the faces of family members who seemed so out of my reach. Johnny, my oldest brother with such a gentle nature was five years my senior. I felt that I barely knew him. Next was Jay's picture, which instantly took me back to the time when we would sleep outside my parents' bedroom door at night whenever they would fight.

Then I came to the picture of Jeff, the brother to whom I was closest not only in age, but also relationally. Gazing at Jeff's image, I recalled how his destructive lifestyle first introduced me to the drug scene. I would often find him down in our basement, dividing pounds of dope into nickel bags, dimes, and lids. I remembered the scales utilized for measuring hash. Jeff told me about *Kief*, a pure form of marijuana. Just two or three hits and the highs were super sensational. Jeff's enticing description was tempting and I responded with a giddy excitement anticipating the time I would say "yes" to this alluring drug. To my surprise, Jeff reacted with an immediate threat. He said, "If you ever touch this stuff, I'll kill you. Do you understand?" I reflected on Jeff's sales ability in pushing drugs at our high school. I both loved him and hated him at the same time.

Peering at the picture of Joel, my youngest sibling, I felt really bad. He was such a good kid to have two brothers that were doing drugs. I wondered how it might impact his future. Finally, I found myself almost hypnotized by the picture of my mom and dad. I asked myself what it would do to them if I carried out my plans. It forced me to think back to the way all my misery began.

The Johnston family fit perfectly into the upper-middle-class stereotype. We lived in Johnson County, Kansas, which at the time was one of the most affluent counties in the nation. My father was quite successful in his position as a national sales director of a company with offices around the country.

My artistic mother was an interior decorator. Our home was a beautiful residence situated next to a golf course. Ours was the country club life.

My life was filled with all the typical self-centered behavior most unruly teenagers manifest. I would get together with my best friend, Bill, and we would do crazy things like interrupt the golf games of the men who regularly played the course, infuriating them. We would gorge ourselves at the clubhouse restaurant and charge it to my parent's account. The only thing I cared about was having fun and moving as fast as possible.

My dad's attempt at forming any kind of real relationships with his five sons was lacking. His way of communicating with me and my brothers was bringing home surprise gifts. Some of the toys we got were an air hockey game, a jukebox, and an electronic bowling machine, among others. Since I was obsessed with things, I took advantage of his spoiling us. One time when he returned from a rather lengthy trip, I woke up and ran downstairs only to discover a brand new motorized mini-bike perfectly positioned on the white carpet of our living room.

I could not talk to my parents about the real issues. They were typical parents—out of touch, antiquated in their thinking, the very epitome of straightness. My dad with his pseudo-religiousness sometimes disgusted me. Mom and Dad were so gullible that they had no idea what I was getting into.

Church was something we participated in on only a few occasions. When we did attend, it was incredibly boring. The minister preached a lifeless, denominationally correct sermon that seemed to lull the frigid congregants to sleep. Even though I knew the official name of the church I couldn't help but refer to it as the First Church of the Deep Freeze. Although I wasn't far off, going to church was the socially acceptable Johnson County thing to do, so we did it. I remember watching my dad taking notes during the sermon. What in the world did he find interesting enough to write down in those little spiral notebooks that filled boxes he stored in his closet?

Occasionally, Dad would convince me to attend the evening youth meeting at church. He would drop me off, but as soon as the taillights of his car left the parking lot, I would leave. One time, a friend and I stole some money from an elderly woman's purse at church, picked up a couple of girls, and left for some real fun.

When the school year began, I sized up the situation almost immediately. There were two dominant self-proclaimed student groups. The "jocks" were the more athletically inclined. They were the drinkers. And then, there were the "freaks," the kids who did drugs and were proud of it. I got involved with the latter group. Every day before and after classes we would hang out at a place right across the street from the school that we creatively called "Across the Street." This was the place you would go before and after the dances at school to do drugs or get drunk. The freaks were a wild bunch of kids, but they made me feel like I belonged and I liked that. Many of the kids would hit on joints until seconds before the final tardy bell rang. None of the faculty ever came over. Some were probably too afraid, but most seemed downright apathetic. More than once I heard snide remarks about "poor little rich kids" and "dumb dopers." And it was all true.

Now I can see that a dangerous rebellion toward authority, particularly toward my parents, began in those days. Maybe it was subliminal from the crowd I hung around. My "friends" were stoners, and they were eager to convert me to their way of living and having fun.

Profanity and offensive speech became my new language. My friends became more important than my "old man" or "old lady"—hard to imagine now that I could have referred to my parents that way. I grew in defiant boldness; fearless to tell my parents to shut up, get out of my room, or leave me alone.

As the weeks passed each new day ended with me adding another brick to the wall I was building between us. Their "fault" was that they were straight, I wasn't, and I condemned them for being so out of touch. I did not want anything to do with them. It was all unfair. In retrospect, I had two of the finest parents a kid could ever want; I just didn't know it at the time.

Living in a world of druggie friends led to serious issues for me at school. I had absolutely no ambition for education so my grades suffered. I mouthed off to one teacher and was permanently ejected from her class. At the all-school, anti-drug assemblies I would sit up in the bleachers and ridicule the speakers. While one expert warned about the horrors of drug addiction, I joked to my friends, "If only we could get that guy high, he would see how much fun he's missing." My disrespectful conduct resulted in me spiraling out of control until finally I got kicked out of five of my seven classes. I was even ejected from study hall—how do you do that?

Five hours a day I occupied a special chair in the school office because of my delinquent behavior. Branded an incorrigible teen, I was told that my days at that particular school were numbered. Near the end of the school year, the principal called my parents in and informed them that I would not be allowed to return to school in the fall. As one would expect, the ride home that day was volcanic. My dad was irate and lectured me the entire time, but his words did not faze me one bit.

The only redeeming thing was that summer was here and that meant I would spend my days and nights hanging around with my friends, and as usual doing nothing constructive. Mostly, we lounged around at the pool and club, smoking, cussing, and condemning anything or anyone that did not match up to our strange standards of coolness. However, in those scarce, contemplative, and quiet moments, I spent time wondering about my new school.

Dad arranged for me to attend a different school that next fall and on the first day of class it was tougher than I expected. As I peered into all those unfamiliar faces while walking down the foreign hallways I felt uneasy and alone. It began to sink in that I knew no one and that I was a nobody in my new surroundings. Anger began to boil up within me as I thought about the principal from my former school. It seemed that he so effortlessly and uncaringly discarded me. I felt sorry for myself, but all that was about to change. I was surprised and thrilled when a tall, blond guy stopped me and boldly introduced himself.

"Hey, I'm Bill. You're new here, aren't you?" His question had all the signs of genuine interest.

"Yeah," I said, "this is my first day—this place is different!"

"Where are you from?" he asked.

I told Bill about being kicked out of my previous school, but left out the sorted details. He only grinned.

"Where do you live?" Bill inquired.

When I answered, "Wycliffe subdivision," his eyes opened wide, and he responded, "Me too. Let's walk home from school together this afternoon." We agreed on a place to meet in front of the school. As I walked away, I thought Bill just might turn out to be a good party buddy. That day the school seemed so straight-laced to me. It was nestled in a quiet residential neighborhood and looked so homey. I figured that the kids at this school weren't nearly as free and easy as the kids from my former school. How wrong I would be.

Moments after the final bell sounded that day, I met Bill outside. As we walked home, he told me about himself. Mincing no words, Bill said he hated his parents, both of whom were alcoholics. They were affluent and successful, but he had no respect for them. His dad was a television announcer with one of our city'ns TV stations and was seldom around. Bill summed up his family situation by saying he lived in a house, not a home. I would soon learn that he was not exaggerating.

That afternoon Bill took a different route from the one I was used to. When I asked him where we were going, he shot back, "Just follow me." I could sense the trepidation in his voice. We went to the front door of a house that had great curb appeal. Bill rang the doorbell. While we waited for someone to answer, I asked, "What are you doing?" He glared at me impatiently and responded, "Shut up. Just pay attention." A cute teenage girl opened the door, and Bill simply stuck out his hand, fist clenched. She extended her hand toward Bill with an open palm, and he gave her some money. "Hold on," she said and disappeared into the house. Within a few moments she returned. Opening the door again, the girl handed Bill several joints, smiled, and said, "Thanks. Have a good time."

Instantaneously, Bill grabbed me by the arm, and we jetted off. Passing through a wooded area, he said, "This is a good place." Bill took out one of the joints, lit it, and began to smoke – inhaling long and then holding it in longer than I had ever seen. I could tell he was studying my reaction. Savoring the first long toke, he said, "Hey, Jerry, you ever been high?"

"No," I said very slowly, yet deliberately.

"Here, hit on this," Bill said as he offered me the joint.

"I don't know." I was a bit hesitant.

"What do you mean, 'I don't know'? C'mon, Jerry, what are you going to do at the Friday and Saturday night parties if you say no?" His question intimidated me, but I observed nervously as he finished.

We stopped by Bill's house, and I was invited in. When we walked into his bedroom, the scene rather shocked me. I couldn't help but be mesmerized by the giant note Bill had written on the wall. He had taken one of those huge smelly permanent markers and written an explicit message to his parents.

Dear Dad & Mom,

You -------. I hate your guts.

Why don't you go -------- on your self?

Get out of my life. Go to hell.

Love, Bill

At home that night I weighed the whole situation. Perhaps I could relate to Bill more than I was willing to admit. My mother was also an alcoholic, but it was the family secret. Everyone knew it, but we all acted oblivious to mom's problem and in the end we were all enablers. Every night mom retired early to her room carrying a glass with vodka in it. I still remember hearing the ice clanging against the glass as she walked past us in her robe as she headed up to her bedroom. She went to bed drunk every night.

I was curious and intrigued about Bill's invitation to take that first hit of marijuana. Part of me wanted to say yes to drugs, but another part of me cried out no! I wanted desperately to tell my dad about what had happened, about this new kid in my life, but I knew better. Dad would have come unglued and totally freaked out. Confiding in him would have only resulted in another major fight. Unable to talk to my parents, that night, I made the decision to try drugs at the next opportunity.

Three days later Bill and I went across the golf course to the house where my girlfriend, Laurie, lived. I knew Laurie well. We used to make out at night on the golf course under the stars. My dad often referred to it as "spooning with the girls." But this day, we were there to see Laurie's sister, Michelle who sold drugs, mainly pot. Bill bought a dime bag and took me behind some trees on the golf course. He reached into his pocket and took out a pipe. Putting a screen in it, he loaded the pipe with the dope. I took in every motion from the striking of the match to the first hit. Then the invitation I had been waiting for came again. Bill stuck the pipe in front of my lips and said, "C'mon. What are you waiting for?"

I coughed as that weed burned into my lungs for the first time. But with a few more tokes, I adjusted. I knew right then that one time would not be enough. Soon, all I cared about was getting high. Before the bus picked me up, during school hours, immediately after school, and always at the parties, I would smoke dope. That pipe became like a trusted friend. I carried the screen to it in my wallet, removing it whenever I had the chance to get a whiff of that can't-wait-until-next-time aroma.

Doing drugs was serious stuff for me and became a staple on weekends. My friends and I would usually go to someone's house for a let's-get-bombed party. The parents, of course, were somewhere else having a party of their own with their friends. Without supervision, there was nothing holding anyone back. Often the goal was not simply pleasure but performance. There was an obsession to outdo the previous week's experience.

One of the preferred things we did was to sit on the floor in a circle, light several joints, put them on roach clips, and pass them around and around. Then, we would try to hit on all of them at once. The goal was to see who could stay in the circle the longest. I can still see my friends and me getting high together and laughing incessantly at any comment that normally would not crack a smile, let alone trigger a laugh.

Tragically, there was more than just marijuana. Somebody would bring alcohol and kids would do drugs and drink—a dangerous combination. Everybody knew we were on the edge, but no one dared to say anything. And there were even worse things. One bizarre practice popular in that era was something called huffing. It involved mainly girls. To huff, a girl would lie flat on the floor while someone straddled her and held a hand towel tightly over her mouth. Another person would then spray an aerosol substance through the towel while the girl inhaled. It gave such a buzz that some girls ended up acting crazy.

At nearly every party, sexual exploits were standard practice. In fact, some parties ended up with what I know now would later result in a lifetime of regrets. The party lifestyle continued for several months, and the goal for me became how many friends I could turn on. I got Bryan, Derek, and other kids into drugs. I wanted them to experience what I tricked myself into believing was ecstasy. Little did I realize when I turned Sandy on to drugs at the bus-stop, she would become an avid user and that several years later she would commit suicide. There are many motivating factors compelling me to reach as many young people as possible through my ministry —but there is no question, the memory of Sandy is a primary one.

At one wild party on a cold spring night, I got high, really high. With my mind reeling, everything was blurred and amplified. Smoking dope can create a strong appetite we called the "munchies." So, I asked Bill to help me find something to eat. He came to my rescue and gave me a full plate of unbaked breakfast rolls and some other junk food. I quickly downed it all without even thinking that I was eating dough.

Just past midnight, Bill's dad picked us up. Sitting in the backseat of their car, I start "coming down." My high was turning into a raunchy low. Mixing the drugs with all that junk food made me feel as if my insides were coming apart. Nauseated, I told Bill, "Man, I don't feel so good." And I vomited all over the backseat. Bill's dad pulled curbside and the car came to a screeching halt, but even before it was fully stopped, Bill flung the door open and threw me out. I lay there on the grassy easement, stunned and sickened. The midnight chill enveloped me and as I attempted to raise my body, my arms were rubbery with weakness. I couldn't move. Bill's dad ordered him to pick me up. He thrust me back into the car for the remaining silent blocks to my house.

It took every ounce of energy for me to make it to the front door. My parents were waiting up for me as I staggered in.

"What's wrong?" they asked.

"Nothing," I said indignantly.

"Are you sick, Jerry?"

"Just leave me alone." Refusing to even look at them, I pushed by and dragged myself up the stairs to my bedroom we affectionately called the Big D. The title held no significance for me and my brother Jeff who shared this space with me.

The following morning I felt no better. In fact, over the next few days I became nauseated every time I ate. When I complained to my mom, she took me to our family doctor. He ran a battery of tests and discovered the source of my problem. I had a bleeding ulcer. The doctor had me hospitalized that same day. I am so glad I became physically sick—I think God used it to save my life!

Laid up in the depressing grayness of that hospital room, I ached with loneliness. The first ones to come see me were some of my druggie friends, but they were not concerned about me as a person. One of them said, "Jerry, you have to get well so you won't miss out on the parties." I thought about that comment, and there for the first time it occurred to me that there was nothing worth living for. You get high; you come down. It is an unending cycle. Drugs don't answer any questions or solve any problems. Instead they just cloud them out temporarily and slowly weaken a person. And, afterward you are still empty, maybe even more so, unfulfilled, searching for something more.

Coming home from the hospital was a strange experience. I wanted things to be better, but I was doubtful they could be. I spent the next several weeks at home attempting to recuperate. Concerned I would fall behind in my studies, my parents hired tutors to come to the house. Our family doctor prescribed Valium and sleeping pills to help me through the recovery period—the very items I would later use in an attempt to end my life. I carried those pill bottles with me constantly in the deep pockets of my dad's light blue bathrobe. To me they felt like a warm security blanket, but they were really an enemy in disguise. I lived in a drug-induced stupor. Already thin from the liquid diet I was on in the hospital, eventually graduating to a bland diet, I lost even more weight. I did no exercise, nor did I want to. By the time I woke up each day, everyone in my family of seven was gone. I was left alone. Awful thoughts continued to plague me. Many times I would hang my head and cry. Did anyone even care about what was happening to me? Did anyone notice? If I did away with myself, everyone would be better off, or so I reasoned. Who wanted to have a sick kid or brother moping around the house every day in his pajamas?

The days were long and without having someone to talk to, depression and hopelessness quickly began to overpower me. Unbeknownst to me, spring was in the air and outside everything was alive and blooming, but inside, I was withering away and dying.

Standing in front of the television on that Friday, April 13, while reviewing the pictures of Mom and Dad and my brothers, I came to my own. *It wouldn't make any difference if you were gone.* The idea seemed so brilliantly simple. Reaching deep into the pocket of Dad's bathrobe, I wrapped my hands tightly around the bottles of pills. The voice in my head in rapid succession said, *"Kill yourself. Do it now. Take the pills and go to bed."* It was late morning. Surely I would be dead before anyone got home. I held the bottles more firmly, as if it was a choice ticket to a big event and I was just about to pass through the turnstile.

Impulsively, I detoured and walked to the kitchen entryway and picked up the telephone receiver. Slowly, mechanically, I called my Dad's office. He answered in typical fashion.

"Johnston," he said gruffly.

Screaming out with tears flowing I announced, "Dad, this is Jerry. I'm going to kill myself."

His immediate response surprised me. I had finally taken the first step toward trusting my Dad for help and his reaction was tender. This tough workaholic father I had come to know broke down at his desk. Suddenly he began to weep over the phone, trying desperately to maintain control.

"Jerry, we'll do something. Son, please hold on. What can I do?"

"Nothing, Dad. It's all over. I'm sorry. My friends are gone. I'm sick. I'm all alone. I'm going to do it."

"Listen, Jerry, I'll be right there. Hold on. I'm coming home now!"

As a parent and grandfather now, I can only imagine the ride home for my dad that day. He later admitted to me that he cried and prayed the entire way as he speedily raced home not sure what condition he would find me in.

Dad's office was downtown and driving the speed limit meant it would take him 30 minutes to get home, but on this morning, it seemed like only a few minutes. When Dad pulled in the driveway and raced into the house I was lying on one of the beds unstable and totally freaking out. Dad gently sat on the edge of the bed and through tears began reasoning with me. I reiterated over and over again, "Please, Dad, do something. Please Dad; make this go away, please." For one hour he desperately tried his best to comfort me. When that failed he finally said, "Jerry let's go. I'm taking you to the hospital." Still wearing his big light blue bathrobe, he gently led me to the car and rushed me to the emergency room of St. Luke's Hospital. To this very day, I can't remember the fifteen minute ride there. I stayed at St. Luke's hospital for over a week, enduring one test after another. The internists were stumped about my condition, since I showed no signs of improvement.

Easter Sunday morning, April 22, I was discharged from the hospital with a checkout weight of only sixty-eight pounds. My parents guided me to the car in the beautiful sunlight on that special Sunday. I peered out the window on the ride home contemplating what the future of my life would hold. Mom and Dad did their best to reassure me that everything was going to be okay. When we rounded the corner pulling up to our house, there waiting for me in the front yard were my four brothers: Johnny, Jay, Jeff, and Joel. Dad had everything prearranged. They were all on their best behavior, treating me as if I were a fragile vase. It was rather strange. I remember us moving the furniture out of the living room when my parents would go out for the evenings and we playing tackle football. We were all boys and although we were rough and tough with each other we all treated my mom rather gently. Nobody wanted to say the wrong thing as I maneuvered out of the car carrying my increasingly skinny body up toward the front door. "Everything is going to be okay, Jerry!" one of my brothers announced.

How I wanted to believe those words. But inside, I was tormented with recurrent thoughts of suicide. Like a pesky fly, the temptation kept buzzing around in my head. Frightened that I might go through with it, I wanted so much to blurt out to my parents the torturous thoughts I was still plagued with. But I couldn't. Everyone was so happy to see me out of the hospital, and my bringing up something negative, let alone s-u-i-c-i-d-e, would ruin the concocted atmosphere. It was all so artificial. Dad was orchestrating as best he could. In his defense, what did he know about a kid wanting to kill himself? At that time, little was said or taught about recognizing suicidal behavior. Within a few years America would start to record a surge in suicides among youth. My suicidal condition was early in the death-wish contagion that would later become so widespread. So, on that sunny Easter Sunday with all the dark clouds and thoughts lurking in my mind, I played along.

I spent eleven long weeks attempting to recuperate. Trapped inside our home I felt like a mental and physical invalid. I became a hypochondriac. I just knew every day I was going to get sick and developed an extremely odd paranoia about vomiting. Those creepy thoughts of suicide were still there. I fought them by reminding myself that someday soon I'd be enjoying good times with my friends again.

While I struggled to fight my way back to normalcy, something sovereignly and significantly happened, though I did not realize it at the time. My brother Johnny became engaged to Teresa Barnes. Teresa was a refreshingly likable person, and the whole family was pleased with Johnny's choice. She politely invited our family to visit her church. Though we did not belong to that Christian denomination, and even though my dad initially resisted, for the sake of courtesy we eventually attended with her.

For reasons I could not sort through, Teresa's church was different from our church. Though I was still feeling depressed and dejected, I sensed something compelling about the atmosphere there. Even from my seat on the back row, I somehow felt drawn in. One of the kids in the church's youth group spotted me and could read how confused and messed up I was. Unbeknownst to me, a few of the courageous kids approached my dad and asked him if I could go with them to their upcoming annual summer youth camp. Their insistence caused something to click in him. Later that day, dad approached me about the subject.

"Jerry, some of the kids at Teresa's church want you to go to summer camp with them in June." His tone was upbeat, but I could tell he was trying real hard to sound as if he wasn't putting something over on me.

"What kind of camp is it, dad?" I asked, expressing no excitement.

"It's a Christian camp."

I thought my Dad had gone crazy, suggesting something like that to me. "Are you kidding?" "You think I'm going to go for a week to some stupid monastery camp with a bunch of straight Jesus-freaks. No way!"

To me, a Christian was either a Boy Scott or a grandma. My dad knew that I needed to go to that camp, for a lot of reasons. So he decided on a friendly blackmail approach. With my birthday just a few days away on May 12, he bought me an expensive gift and had it delivered in our basement without me knowing it. When he came home later that day, he stopped me and said, "Jerry, I want you to change your mind about going to that camp."

"Drop it. Dad, I said no!"

He just smiled.

"I've got your birthday gift in the basement. Do you want to see it?"

Before I answered, I hurried down the basement stairs to discover what he had bought for me. I couldn't believe it! Right there in my own home was the most beautiful professional foosball table I had ever seen. My friend Bill and I spent hours playing foosball up at the arcade competing against one another. My dad knew how much I enjoyed the game. I had already reached the table and was spinning the handles in anticipation of hours of fun when he dropped the bombshell.

"That's your birthday present … if you go to that camp. If

not, I'll have it taken back."

I knew my dad well enough to realize he wasn't kidding. In the exhilaration of the moment, I reluctantly agreed. In the blink of an eye, on June 18, I found myself leaning against a station wagon in the parking lot of Teresa's church getting ready for the drive down to Lake-of-the-Ozarks, Missouri to a camp called Windermere. I felt really odd and out of place with those church kids. Hoping I wouldn't get sick on the three hour drive, I grasped my pill bottles and managed to get into the right front passenger seat and sat quiet and withdrawn for the long drive.

The camp wasn't nearly as bad as I had predicted. I was surprised to discover that there were a lot of interesting things to do. I was the loner, but unbeknownst to me, I had attracted the attention of some pretty cool looking older kids. Every night they had a meeting in an auditorium, and I made sure to sit on the back row. It began with the kids singing some songs I had never heard so I just stoically watched while everybody sang. This routine went on for four days and on the last night of camp, June 21, a very attractive girl named Cindy walked from the front of the auditorium all the way to the back row where I was parked, offered her hand and said, "Jerry, come sit with me. I want you to hear the message tonight." I wasn't so enthused about hearing the "message," but she was so gorgeous I could not refuse.

As I walked to the front of the auditorium, I'm sure I was quite a sight. Long flowing blonde hair and I was wearing my favorite jeans (which also served as my pajamas). I had a girlfriend sew a large chicken claw patch on the rear of one of my back pockets. Everyone thought it was a marijuana patch. Some of the counselors looked as if they were going to have a heart attack when I took my seat on the second row.

I fully planned to use the time to get more acquainted with Cindy. Instead, I experienced the greatest miracle of my life that night. The speaker spoke for an hour, and I was absolutely captivated. In a firm, powerful way he told a story I had never heard. Because I listened to him and acted on his challenge, that night my life was revolutionized! Almost spontaneously, I raced back to my cabin, walked over to the toilet while opening the lids to my pill bottles and watched as every one of them individually dropped into the water. Overjoyed I flushed them away forever and immediately felt renewed.

An upperclassman who I had come to know owned a cool sports car that he had driven to camp that week. I was thrilled when he invited me to ride back home with him the next morning in his awesome Camaro. Like me, he had also had a life change that week and we were both celebrating as we hurriedly sped home. I went home a radically different person. The confusion and craziness that overpowered me was gone. I started to think straight. I started to live right. I began to grow from that night on in my understanding of what life is all about. My parents almost passed out when I burst through the front door after camp upon my return and exclaimed, "Dad, Mom, I'm changed. I feel so good! Something happened at camp and I don't want to kill myself anymore. There is no more depression. I want to live!" Their first reaction was, "Son, what are you up to now?" But, within moments they broke down crying and have been shedding tears of joy ever since.

Later on, I will tell you what the camp speaker said that historic evening. But, first let's examine the subject of suicide. Together we will take a look at the causes, the misconceptions, and the warning signs. And I will zero in on specific courses of action to help people who may be contemplating suicide.

CHAPTER 2

Warning Signs

*The most common health disorder is depression
with over 25 percent (1 in 4) affected by mild symptoms.
It is these young people that are at the
highest risk for committing suicide.*

"I can't believe it. She just wasn't the type of person you'd expect to commit suicide. There weren't any signs at all." I have lost count of the number of times I have heard this expression as I sit with parents who told me about the suicide of their child. The problem is, that it is simply not true. Suicide is a problem or set of problems or motivated impulses that gestates with time and ultimately erupts, generally, after some type of trigger mechanism. Often, that trigger is some final disappointment, a state of perceived hopelessness that sends a person over the edge.

When a parent or grandparent says to me, "There was no indication of anything wrong. There was no clue as to a deep need. No sign of a serious problem," I must confess, I always raise my eyebrows in disbelief because seldom does a teenager or adult commit suicide without giving some warning. My extensive research has borne this out, and my conversations with many who have attempted suicide and family members and friends of a loved one who has completed suicide reinforce this conviction. A spokesperson for the Suicide and Crisis

Center in Dallas, says 80 percent of teenagers have given one or more signs of their intention beforehand. There *are* warning sign—deadly giveaways that say a teenager is potentially suicidal. Knowing them can prevent a tragedy. But keep in mind that there is not one exclusive type of suicidal person, and different individuals will express the same warning signs differently. Some signs relate to what a person does, others to what a person doesn't do.

> *1. Withdrawal—the teen that pulls away.* To a certain extent, withdrawal is natural and good during the teenage years. Developing healthy independence equips a teen for successful adulthood. But when withdrawal is severe, when there is an obvious pulling away and into a shell, watch out.

Daily sensitivity is the key to recognizing negative withdrawal. Unfortunately, our frenetic, contemporary lifestyle often desensitizes us. Social media can help insulate a young person particularly when they are depressed and have suicidal ideation. Without knowing it, we can find ourselves more interested in the families on TV sitcoms than in our own. One counselor points out that some families where a hectic, busy pace is kept and family members do not give much attention, withdrawal may not be noticed. In fact, in some families, far too often, withdrawal may even be welcomed.

Unwillingness to communicate is perhaps the most common form of withdrawal, but there are other telltale indicators. Failing grades can express a withdrawal from school. A broken teenage romance can be a catalyst to withdrawal. The divorce of parents can cause kids to withdrawal. Rejection of normally pleasurable activities such as sports or hobbies may suggest a self-punishing type of withdrawal. I know of students who made a suicide attempt when they were cut from the varsity football or hockey team, the school play, and other athletic activities. And an incessant desire to be alone can also spell a disaster in the making. Make sure your children or grandchildren are not pulling away and if they are, notice it!

> *2. Moodiness—the teen who is up and down.* Everyone is moody from time. We are all influenced by the weather, our health, our circumstances, and social relationships in life. Teenagers are no different.

But when there are wide shifts in personality and emotional make-up, up one day and rock-bottom the next, there is cause for concern and alarm. One expert observed that sudden, inexplicable euphoria or whirlwind activity after a spell of gloom means danger. There is ample evidence to conclude that many teens have ridden an emotional roller coaster to death. Let me give you an example, we have documented cases of youth suicide where a teen formerly withdrawn becomes gregarious, unpredictably and artificially happy. It is a "live it up I am going to die soon" mentality. Conversely, we have also noted students who were formerly conversational, outgoing, and engaging who become silent and withdrawn. When the pendulum swings noticeably in a prominent new and different direction for the young person you know, take notice and do something. Moodiness is closely associated with the next two warning signs.

> *3. Depression—the teen that holds in.* Depression is a highly individualized experience. Some teenagers when they are depressed, become very sullen and totally wrapped up in themselves. Others camouflage their feelings so well that no one is aware anything is happening. In such cases, the only way to find out is by somehow getting the person to talk.

Health Canada reminds us of the key areas where a person can become depressed: the death or illness of someone close, difficulties at work or with a personal friendship, low self-esteem, financial difficulties, and addictions.[1] The National Institute of Health Care Management in Washington, DC remind us that students with unidentified mental disorders are in poorer physical health and engage in more risky behaviors like unsafe sexual activity, fighting and weapon carrying. The most common mental health disorder is depression with over 25 percent (1 in 4) affected by mild symptoms. It is these young people that are at the highest risk for committing suicide.[2] Understanding how depression develops can be beneficial. Dr. Tim LaHaye theorizes that nearly always it is the result of anger combined with self-pity. The anger may be due to a failure, an unrealized expectation, or a personal loss. As the emotions focus on whatever prompted the anger, feelings of self-pity follow.[3] Self-pity can give way to suicidal thoughts: Nobody understands what I am going through. There's no way I can get out of this situation.

> **4. Aggression—the teen that lashes out.** Many suicide attempts are preceded by violent outbursts—fights, threats, cruel insults, even destruction of property. Frequently, acts of this nature are cries for help. But this kind of aggressive behavior, though usually out of character, often achieves the opposite result: rejection rather than consideration. The teenager who wanted to be noticed is condemned instead.

Look no further than the Aurora, Colorado theatre massacre with James Holmes. He had been a PhD student in neuroscience at the University of Colorado Anschutz Campus. Obviously, James knew he had a problem. He met with not one, but at least three mental health professionals at the University of Colorado prior to the shooting noticed something was off. Dr. Lynne Fenton, a psychiatrist at the school, was so concerned about Holmes' behavior she contacted the university's threat assessment team nearly six weeks before Holmes opened fire in a crowded theatre. Prosecutors claim Holmes "had conversations with a classmate about wanting to kill people in March 2012, and that he would do so when his life was over," attorneys for the state wrote.[4] Nothing was done in time to intervene in Holmes' maniacal condition.

Dylan Klebold, one of the killers in the Columbine high school shooting, wrote in his diary, "People are so unaware … well, ignorance is bliss, I guess … that would explain my depression."[5] His sad diary continues, "I don't fit in. I've been thinking of suicide gives no hope, that I'll be in my place wherever I go after this life … that I'll finally not be at war with myself, the world, the universe—my mind, body." Helped by his accomplice, Eric Harris, this depressed duo killed twelve students and injured 24 others, before taking their own lives. As a parent, would you not demand to see the school paper your son had written about a mass murder. I have a hard time accepting the gullibility of Sue Harris, Dylan's mom, who 10 years later wrote in O Magazine:

> These thoughts may seem foolish in light of what we know now, but they reflect what we believed to be true about Dylan. Yes, he had filled notebook pages with his private thoughts and feelings, repeatedly expressing profound alienation. But we'd never seen those notebooks. And, yes, he'd written a school paper about a man in a black trench coat who brutally murders nine students. But we'd never seen the paper. (Although it had alarmed his English teacher enough to bring it to our attention, when we asked to see the paper at a parent-teacher conference, she didn't have it with her … we agreed that she would show the paper to Dylan's guidance counselor; if he thought it was a problem, one of them would contact me. I never heard from them.)[6]

Respectfully, I don't buy it. If your son had written an essay about killing nine classmates at school would you not have demanded to see the paper? In the same article Mrs. Klebold says after the Columbine murders, she started to learn all she could about suicide. That is good, but it is too late. In the infamous "basement tapes" both Klebold and Harris record and boast about concocting their plan under the noses of their unsuspecting parents and friends. Dylan is quoted on the tapes, and refers to the teenager who he gunned down just outside the school, Rachel Scott. He calls her a "godly little whore."[7] Harris kept the shotgun he used in the killings in the closet in his bedroom. These troubled friends planned this massacre for months.

A less-obvious form of presuicidal aggression is risk-taking. This could include recklessness with motor vehicles or participation in dangerous activities. An eighteen-year-old boasted that a death wish motivated him to take up skydiving and wing walking on airplanes. In counseling it was discovered that he was trying to get the attention of his father who ignored him.

>*5. Alcohol and drug abuse—the teen that turns on.* Alcohol and drugs are always an escape, but especially for the teenager with life-ending thoughts. Sudden indulgence by a young person who had not previously abused alcohol or experimented with drugs is a definite red flag.

>*6. Sexual activity—the teen that lets go.* Inappropriate sexual behavior sometimes reflects a desperate desire to relieve depression. By letting go completely with another person, the depressed teenager thinks satisfaction can finally be achieved. When there is no lasting satisfaction, suicidal thoughts can and often do intensify.

>*7. Eating disorders—the teen who punishes self.* Anorexia and bulimia are words now well known by most people in North America. These frightful diseases have a strong connection to self-destructive thoughts and should always be considered potentially suicidal. Concerned friends and family members should watch for drastic weight loss. Karen Carpenter, whose soothing voice worked its way into the hearts of

millions of people, died of an anorexia-induced heart attack and is a potent example of the risk. Hers was an unintentional suicide.

8. *Gift giving—the teen who gives up and gives away.* Some young people who plan to take their lives will give away prized possessions to close friends or to other they wish were close friends. Suicide experts say this is an ominous action, a silver cloud with a very dark lining. It should prompt serious, concerned questioning. I have had parents of children who committed suicide tell me that in retrospect that should have known. It was so obvious and well planned. Regretfully, again, it is awareness too late.

9. *Trauma—the teen that's been hit hard.* Each person has an emotional threshold, an internal breaking point. A major traumatic event or series of circumstances can drive a teenager closer and closer to that edge. A family moves to another community or city can seem like the end of the world to a young person who has built strong ties and sunk deep roots. The trauma of a divorce, a death, and an accident – any such experience can hit a teenager hard, leaving the young person stunned with thoughts of suicide running through their mind. And, remember, one of the most significant traumas a teenager can experience is the suicide of a friend of family member. Suicidologists refer to this phenomenon as a *contagion affect.* Rarely do we hear of just one teen suicide in a school, community, or multigenerational in a family. When a person commits suicide, to a close friend or family member it can induce not only feelings of guilt and sorrow but actually prompt personal problems to a perceived abnormal level. In North America, we have experienced scores of communities that registered as suicide clusters. A few decades ago the media would play up adolescent suicides and it had a tragic perpetuating effect. The U.S. government made recommendations to media to discourage the emotional retelling of youth suicides and there has been a notable change in media coverage. Youth suicide still occurs at alarming levels. In fact, in both the United States and Canada, youth suicide is on the rise. But, we don't read the in-depth personal stories with the exception of celebrities as we use to. There is a reason why, and this type of responsible journalism recognizes there are more potential suicides waiting to happen, which warrants restraint and responsibility.

10. Personality change—the teen that's not the same. Abrupt reversal is the thing to watch for. When a usually introverted person suddenly begins to act like an unbridled extrovert, joking and carrying on, it's not a laughing matter. Conversely, this holds true as well when the gregarious person becomes a silent loner. Personality change is also expressed in a lessened energy level, neglect of responsibility, elimination of personal ambition, or an I-don't-care attitude toward personal appearance. Don't be afraid to intervene when you see these noticeable personality changes.

11. Threat—the teen that speaks out. Any comment regarding the desire to die should always be taken seriously. Some of the most common threats are "I wish I'd never been born" or "You're going to be sorry when I'm gone" or "I want to go to sleep and never wake up." These should be interpreted as seriously as "I'm going to kill myself."

As I have mentioned repeatedly, diligently watch for these signs. Don't feel helpless, because you're not. You can help a suicidal person. You must communicate openly with the person, asking questions to probe the troubled individual's conscience. You must empathize, not being judgmental or harsh, but not being overly sympathetic either. And you *must* act! In the following pages I will give more specific guidelines on what you can do.

CHAPTER 3

Common Myths About Suicide

The exponential impact on the immediate family and friends of each person who commits suicide reveals that this traumatizes thousands of people each year.

Worldwide 1,000,000 people take their lives each year—a staggering number! Every fifteen minutes someone commits suicide in the United States. More U.S. citizens kill themselves than kill one another every year! In fact, that is twice as many suicides as murders. One in five suicides in the United States is a war veteran. Native American/Alaska Native youth have the highest rate of suicide with 14.8 suicides per 100,000. White youth are next highest with 7.3 deaths per 100,000. Males take their lives at nearly five times the rate of females and represent more than 80 percent of all U.S. suicides.[8] Women, however, during their lifetime attempt suicide about two to three times more often than that of men. In a recent interview with Dr. Alex Crosby, foremost expert on youth suicide and medical epidemiologist at the Centers for Disease Control in Atlanta, Georgia, shared with me the growing trend of young females to commit suicide by hanging. It is something of a mystery the CDC is studying. We spent an hour discussing the realities and implications of teen suicide. Suicide rates for females are highest among those aged 45-54. And there is an increased number of suicides among middle age men. At present time poisoning is the most common method of suicide for females. Firearms are the most commonly used method of suicide among males.[9] Suicide is the second-leading cause of death among college students, and the third-leading cause of death among those aged 15-24 years. It is the fourth-leading cause of death among those aged 10-14 years.[10] We would refer to these deaths as completed suicides, and for every person who takes their life there are 25 attempted suicides.[11] The National Institute of Mental health even documents a six-year-old who killed himself! The exponential impact of each person who commits suicide on their immediate family and friends reveals this traumatizes multiplied thousands of people each year.

Tony stood next to me at one of our events and asked that I read a statement to the few thousand teens that assembled in the auditorium. The reason I was reading his thought-provoking words was because, in his attempt to kill himself with a gun, Tony blew most of his face literally off his head. His girlfriend, Missy, had heard me speak in her public school and told me about his horrific situation. I followed up and went to see him. We developed a friendship of trust. In his suicide attempt the gunshot removed Tony's nose, most of his face under his eyes, his mandible bone, and the majority of his teeth. Plastic surgeons formed two slits for air holes in replacement of his nose so he could breathe and closed most of his mouth. Tony was fed directly into his stomach. I am reluctant to write and say that just looking at him was a frightful sight. This is the other side of suicide; most young people who romanticize with suicidal ideation rarely think about the consequences of a failed attempt. Only after impairing himself so dramatically did Tony realize what a priceless gift life truly is. He wants to live now more than ever and faces years of excruciatingly painful surgeries in hopes of trying to look human again. You can imagine how frozen that youth audience was as I recited Tony's words telling them to stay off drugs and make wise decisions as he penetratingly stared at them.

I have personally seen many people who tried to kill themselves and did not complete suicide. Remember, no one is ever successful at suicide! In a way, I wish I could take each student flirting with death by abusing drugs and alcohol and have them join me at the besides of these dear people who physically and mentally impaired themselves the rest of their lives because of their death wish. Candidly, it is not that easy to kill yourself. Imagine being depressed, suicidal, make the attempt, and then waking up to find out you are paralyzed; can't speak, walk, or see. It happens innumerable times every year. People become prisoners within their inoperable bodies. We now hear of "psychological autopsies." Tragically and belatedly, parents, counselors, psychiatrists, mental health experts work to put together a composite of the emotional and psychological disorders of someone who has completed suicide. But in a sense it is too late—the data helps us with other potential victims.

Suicide is the second leading cause of death among teenagers in Canada. Experts warn that the beginning of the school term is a perilous time. As in the United States, more Canadian young men complete suicide but four times as many Canadian young girls attempt suicide. Shockingly, Canada's youth-suicide rate per capita is nearly triple that of the United States. In part this is explained by the high suicide rates in the Canadian native communities. The age-standardized mortality rate in Nunavut, the fifth-largest country subdivision in the world and a major part of Northern Canada, is the highest in Canada at 51.2 suicides per 100,000 people; a rate that is 3-6 times higher than the rate in other provinces/territories. The suicide rate in males is over four and a half times the rate of females![12] The number of girls committing suicide in Canada has risen in the past 30 years, a troubling trend that is prompting some experts to question the interplay of social media. Another concerning shift is the way young people are killing themselves. Researchers noted a decrease in suicide from poisoning or firearms. Suffocation, which includes hanging and strangulation, is now the predominant method of suicide among children and adolescents in a study published in 2012 Canadian Medical Association Journal, using data of researchers from the Public Health Agency of Canada. And, as studies have proved in other areas, it is equally true that marriage is a deterrent to suicide. In general, married people were the least likely to commit suicide compared with single, widowed or divorced individuals. Statistics Canada, reports hangings have been the most common method of suicide since 1992, but it was used less often at older ages.[13]

Social media makes it easier than ever for young people to share their thoughts and connect with others, which isn't always a positive thing. Cyber bullying, when people receive hurtful and even threatening messages online, has become a serious problem across Canada. There are also countless websites where users can share suicidal thoughts and even instructions on methods to kill themselves. That is why I insist on parents being included—in not only their children's social networking sites, but also their children's friends' sites so they can see if someone has posted any odd messages. This, too, is an excellent way to discover if your son or daughter is the victim of bullying. Text messages may be more difficult to know about, so parents should try to keep up communication with their children about bullying. In several cases where bullying victims killed themselves, bullies had told the teen that he or she should kill him or herself and that the world would be better without them. Parents who see a serious bullying problem should talk to school authorities about it, and perhaps arrange a meeting with the bully's parents. More states are implementing laws against bullying, and recent lawsuits against schools and criminal charges against bullies show that there are legal avenues to take to deal with bullies. If school authorities do not help with an ongoing bullying problem, local police or attorneys will be able to.

Before you finish reading this chapter, several teenagers throughout North America will try to kill themselves. Just one life lost is one too many. The deaths will make news for a day, and then be forgotten by the public. Family, friends, and acquaintances will be left in the aftermath groping through a dense fog of uncertainty. They will wonder, evaluate, and ask time and again, "Why did they die? Why did they commit suicide?" The doubts will lead to speculation, and the speculation will lead to wrong conclusions. I say this with certainty because I have seen it happen so frequently. Misconceptions about suicide are prevalent.

Many people are hesitant to even discuss the subject of suicide. I can distinctly remember teachers, principals, pastors, and priests who would express fear that if I talked about suicide it would cause suicides. Nothing could be further from the truth, as every suicidologist and mental health worker knows. Thankfully, much of that ignorant attitude and sentiment has dissipated across North America but more work needs to be done to eliminate the common myths about suicide.

Let me clearly state my opinion in this chapter that I am convinced most of our statistics regarding suicide (at least in the United States) are inaccurate. Follow my argument. As we are aware, there is a certain amount of death certificate error and bias with some suicides. The statistics collected and reported by the CDC are from deaths that are indisputably recognized as suicides. Ironically, many alcohol and drug related deaths are not certified as a suicide, therefore, not in our totals. Also, we know that a number of affluent families want to avoid the stigma of suicide and this, too, influences the registry at death. In addition, there are theological implications for some faiths if a person commits suicide. In certain faith systems it equates to instant damnation. This bias influences "cause of death" on the cases where it is not an indisputably recognized suicide, and sometimes even if it is. The collecting of data from coroners across the country is not always efficient and comprehensive. Every case of morbidity, which finds its way in to the sorting categories of death registered at the Centers for Disease Control and Prevention is highly doubtful. What about the accuracy of rural America? What about the thousands of missing persons in the U.S. who are never accounted for? How many alcohol related crashes were disguised suicides? How many drug induced deaths, like Michael Jackson, were simply people who had lost the will to live? And, what of the multiplied thousands of family members and close friends who develop mental, and emotional problems, and even experience early death due to the grief of the suicide of someone they loved dearly? Perhaps Canada has a much more comprehensive surveillance system due to its population compared to the United States. If you think the numbers of suicides are alarming, and indeed they are, I think we would be quite shocked if we knew the actual quantity of people who are committing suicide annually, a much higher number indeed.

You, too, probably have some false ideas about suicide. I know I did. So, once and for all, let's set the record straight on several key points. Let's dispel some commonly held myths about suicide.

Myth #1—People who talk about suicide don't commit suicide. Wrong. Dead wrong. Dr. Edwin Schneidman, respected for his knowledge in the field, reminds us that the notion that people who talk about suicide don't do it is the most dangerous myth in the world. Four out of five suicides have made previous attempts and in every single instance the person gives clues, warning signals, that he or she is about to do it.

What if a suicidal person dares to talk to you about self-destructive thoughts? How will you respond? Many people, often parents in particular, out of fear and ignorance, refuse to get involved. Wrongly, they think that by discussing suicide with the suicidal person the risk will heighten. Not so. By expressing those morbid thoughts, the suicidal person is saying, "Help me! I'm trying to get a handle on this!"

Let me give you a strategy of compassion, concern, and intervention. If someone you know is exhibiting any of the warning signs of suicidal ideation I recommend the following:

- *Listen and observe the person very carefully.* Don't do all the talking and certainly don't preach at a hurting person. Emotions are raw when a person is suicidal. Think of how gently you would respond to someone if they had a broken arm, wrist, or leg. Now approach the person *emotionally* with the same care, quietness, and attentiveness. Ask the suicidal person to explain to you what is bothering them. Be aware they may not have the ability to articulate their problem(s) like a used car salesman. Let them talk. Look into their eyes. Stay quiet and listen. Remember, too, that when a teenager or spouse is abusing drugs or alcohol they are talking to you by their behavior. The abuse of drugs and alcohol is a person telling you, "I am in pain. I have to medicate myself because I am hurting." For you to simply watch their addiction grow more severe year after year makes you an enabler of the worst kind. My mother was alcoholic my entire childhood. Joyce never said she wanted to kill herself. But, Mom was drinking herself to death. I knew she was going to die if my four brothers and I did not do something about her degenerating condition. To make a long story short, one prearranged night my brothers with me serving as the ringleader, unannounced, came to my parents home, physically picked up my Mom and took her to a local hospital and force-checked her in against her will. I remember how angry she was at me! Our drastic action literally saved her life. Mom has been alcohol free for nearly 25 years. I tell parents, "Don't tell me you love your son or daughter when you know they are doing drugs or alcohol or running with the wrong people who are killing them, and you do nothing about it." That is not love. That is being an enabler. Shame on you. People who are suicidal are depending upon us to notice, care, and do something about their troubled condition! Listen, listen, listen, and keep listening.

• *Identify with the hurting person.* If your son, daughter, wife, husband, or friend tells you they have been thinking about ending their life don't look at them like they are some kind of freak. Again, don't preach a sermon to them; telling the person that if he/she was a good Christian, they would not be thinking suicidal thoughts. Jonah asked God to kill him. Elijah did the same, and they were prophets of God. Disobedient Saul killed himself. Judas hung himself. Identify with the hurting person. Suicidologists remind us of something many starchy, self-righteous Christians often forget. Most people, at some point in their life, have had a fleeting to serious thought about ending their life. Admit it. I told you my story in this book. Since the time when I was a teenager I have faced a number of particularly challenging days when I did not think I could go on. I loved God. I loved my wife Cristie. I loved my three kids and their spouses. I loved my grandchildren. Simultaneously, I was simply overwhelmed. It is called life. And, thankfully, I have had three key people in my life who have always been there to listen and observe me very carefully.

• *Initiate a loving, calculated response (be very, very*

careful). Here is a hypothetical conversation between a father we will call Sam and his 17-year-old son, Kelly, who has been morose and dejected. Sam knows his kid is in trouble. He has pillow talked the concern for his boy to his wife night after night. Sam could approach his son: Kelly, you have been acting as though you have been down lately, are you? (Wait for a response.) Kelly, did you know that your dad has had times in his life when he has been depressed, too? In fact, Kelly, there were times I did not know if I could go on. Are you having similar thoughts?

• *Ask the key question.* Whenever we suspect that someone near and dear to us is contemplating taking his or her life there is an essential question that must be asked. *Do you have a plan or method to take your life? Have you considered an actual time to do it?* Whenever a person has logically thought out a plan or method to commit suicide and associated a specific timetable to it, they are in immediate danger. They should never be left alone. You must get that suicidal person to a trained professional who has expertise in diagnosing the situation and making specific recommendations for help and healing. This may require a hospitalization; the expertise of a reputable counselor, psychiatrist, or trained, experienced pastor who can intervene. Don't get in over your head—seek help from someone truly qualified. I have had actual counseling experiences with young people where I would not end the session without privately calling the adolescent's parents and telling them I was convinced their child was at high risk and needed to be hospitalized. I've been engaged in this work long enough to know there is no room for error. On one occasion I happened to make a house call and after repeated knocks on the door, no one came to answer. Yet, through the window I could see the youth I had come to see sleeping peacefully on the couch in the living room. It didn't make sense. I was making enough noise to easily wake him up, and yet he did not move. Something or Someone compelled me to crawl through an unlock window allowing me entrance inside the home where I discovered the young man had taken 36 Quaaludes and was almost dead! I rode in the ambulance and watched with the greatest grief as paramedics feverishly pumped the boy's stomach on the way to the hospital. Miraculously, he lived. What if I would have left that front door and assumed he was just in a deep sleep? Don't be afraid to intervene when you know someone who is sending out cries for help.

Myth #2—Suicides usually happen without warning. No, suicides do not occur unpredictably. They are more often than not the result of long-term inner struggle that is expressed outwardly in some clearly recognizable actions and attitudes. There is almost always a clue, usually several, that a person is suicidal. A suicidal person shows signs of depression, like ongoing sadness, withdrawal from others, losing interest in favorite activities, or trouble sleeping or eating. It is not uncommon to notice a preoccupation with death or death themes and showing an interest in dying. The engagement in deliberately dangerous or harmful activities, including reckless behavior, substance abuse, or self-injury is other warnings exhibited. Frequent expressions like, "I can't handle this any more," or "I am so tired of living" should be taken as a verbal warning. A suicidal person will exhibit:

- Feelings of hopelessness or worthlessness, depression and low self esteem or guilt

- Not wanting to participate in family or previous social activities

- Again, a marked change may occur in sleeping or eating patterns

- Feelings of rage, anger, need for revenge

- No energy, lethargy
- Poor academic performance, quitting a job or school
- Multiple emotional outbursts or the sheer absence of emotion
- Lack of hygiene and self care, letting themselves go
- Excessive abuse of drugs or alcohol
- Sexual promiscuity or lack of interest in sex
- Comments on physical symptoms of discomfort

Myth #3—Suicidal people can't be talked out of it if they are really intent on dying. Dr. Schneidman again provides direction, "Nonsense! [A suicidal person] is in a state of confusion and irrational thinking; he wants to continue to his life but can't see the way. We find so frequently that lethal drives last just a short time so that if you can get him through the period of severe stress, his entire outlook can change and the very next day he may no longer be the slightest bit suicidal." [14]

Nearly every suicidal person is torn between living and dying to such an extent that one authority says the leap off a building may be the tragic result of a 51 to 49 internal vote. For concerned friends, this wavering between two sides is an opportunity to speak up and reach out.

Myth #4—An individual's improvement following a suicidal crisis means the suicide risk is over. Paul tried to hang himself because, as he put it in a terse note to his parents:

Nobody loves me. Nobody really talks to me. They just throw words at me.

Paul survived, however, and he seemed to be making improvement. "I thought he had solved his problem," said his father. But Paul made a second attempt four months after the first. Help arrived too late. His final note read:

Nobody listens. They say, "How are you?" and that's about as far as it goes. I don't want to live in a world where it hurts so bad inside all the time.

Paul's case, unfortunately, is tragically typical. The person most likely to complete suicide is one who failed in a previous attempt. Of all the signs, this one is the most foreboding. The parent or friend's role in this circumstance is to act, not assume. Saying, "I thought he was getting better" will not bring the person back. After a failed attempt, it is imperative to show you care by spending time daily with the person, talking, doing things together, enjoying life, and insuring that the person who has attempted suicide is regularly being counseled by someone qualified, i.e., a mental health therapist, a trained counselor or experienced pastor.

Myth #5—Suicide strikes more often among the rich. I like what N. L. Farberow says about this, "Suicide is neither the rich man's disease nor the poor man's curse."[15] In fact, suicide is very democratic and includes a proportionate number of victims from all levels of society. Another study indicates that the average person who commits suicide is close to the average person.

Myth #6—Suicide is hereditary; it runs in families. There is absolutely no evidence to suggest suicidal tendencies are hereditary. We do know some mental illnesses are multigenerational, and we can assuredly attribute some suicides to mental illness. Also, there is unquestionably a powerful negative influence on surviving families when a suicide occurs. One psychiatrist calls it survivor's guilt—a curious belief that the "wrong person" died. A confused teenager told me, "My father was such a good man. He never hurt anybody and worked so hard for the family. Look at me. I'm a mess, and I keep screwing up in everything I do. Why am I the one still alive?"

When a family member takes his or her own life, it can

prompt suicidal thoughts and even a suicide attempt among the survivors. This is especially true of a person already deeply troubled. But none of this has anything to do with genetic factors. No one is doomed to act a certain way or destined to end it all because a family member made a fateful decision.

Myth #7—Someone who commits suicide is mentally ill. Marcia attempted suicide when she was fifteen and again at seventeen. In her own words she told why:

The agony and the confusion at the time seemed permanent. My main concern was that if the situation I was in was going to be permanent, I wanted no part of it. That death would be permanent was of no consideration to me. There is a great feeling of being hopeless and lost and your self-image is in pretty bad shape when you're thinking about suicide.

Marcia, I am convinced, is not mentally ill. She is quite normal and, thankfully, quite alive today. But she does illustrate the severity of adjustment during the teenage years. Like the butterfly freeing itself from the cocoon, the teenager must stretch new emotional muscles before finally breaking. It is a wonderful, difficult time, and there are many obstacles along the way. Kids tell me about their pain, their feelings of rejection, and the ugly suspicion that no one really cares. But they are not insane. Let me say, there are mental illnesses which contribute to completed suicides, but not all people who complete suicide are mentally ill. I am aware some psychiatrists might debate me on this point. It has been my observation that people who are not mentally ill, and have had no history of mental illness, have made a suicide attempt or completed suicide due to the problems and complications in their life.

Some very bright young people take their lives because they no longer want to mask the secret torment that lurks inside. A prominent medical journal reported its finding that 12 percent of grade-school children, age six to twelve years, have had suicidal ideas or made suicidal threats. Are these children crazy? No. Are they vulnerable? You better believe they are.

Myth #8—Only young people commit suicide in significant numbers. Suicide is the third leading cause of death for U.S. teenagers and second leading cause of death for Canadian teens. However, older Americans are disproportionately more likely to die by suicide. Of every 100,000 people, ages 65 and older, 14.3 died by suicide in 2007 in the U.S. This figure is higher than the national average of 11.3 suicides per 100,000 people in the general population.[16]

Myth #9—Women threaten suicide, but men carry it out. This myth comes from a misinterpreted fact. As stated early, five times as many men as women complete suicide, but two to three times as many women attempt suicide. The explanation for this phenomenon lies in the suicide method. Historically, women choose less violent methods to die by suicide such as pills or poison, increasing the chance of rescue. When I asked Dr. Crosby at the CDC why there is now a slow reversal of this trend with adolescent girls who have been dying by hanging he answered, "We're not sure." The CDC continues to probe this mystery as with many other mysterious aspects of suicide.

Myth #10—Talking about suicide causes suicide by planting the idea in a person's head. I am amazed at how widespread this myth really is! In years past, I have had some critics claim that I inadvertently encourage teenagers to commit suicide by addressing the topic. Every suicidologist will adamantly deny that by talking about suicide or confronting individuals who have a suicidal ideation it causes suicides. The opposite is true. I know many young people are already thinking about suicide, and they are often convinced no one has ever felt or cared about the way they feel. By talking about suicide and by identifying causal reasons and the feelings they are experiencing, we are bringing everything out in the open. Just knowing that others are struggling, too, helps immeasurably in a teenager's ability to cope. No, talking about suicide will not cause suicide. But failing to talk about it may have disastrous consequences.

- Talking about suicide will plant the idea in a depressed person's mind. True/**False**

- People who talk about suicide usually do not follow through with it. True/**False**

- Most suicides occur without warning. True/**False**

- If there is no note, it was not a suicide. True/**False**

- When depression lifts, suicide is no longer a concern. True/**False**

- A suicidal person cannot be talked out of it if he/she is intent on dying. True/**False**

- Women threaten suicide, but only men complete suicide. True/**False**

- Only certain people are the suicidal type. True/False

- African American men complete suicide at the same quantities as Caucasian men. True/**False**

- Only insane or "crazy" people complete suicide. True/**False**

- If a person has survived a suicide attempt the likelihood of a second attempt is diminished. True/**False**

- People who complete suicide have not sought medical help prior to the attempt. True/**False**

CHAPTER 4

Coach Don and Dylan

"Friends, its time to put our anchors down.
Good bye Dyl."

In God's plan and sovereignty, and at the request of Crossroads' founder, David Mainse, I was asked to become the Chairman and CEO of this reputable fifty-year ministry. Crossroads has faithfully used media technology to present the love of God and the life altering relationship to be found in Him, to millions of people. I believe strongly that we need to use the powerful influence of the media to counteract its hold on our culture. It is an honour to apply my business experience and knowledge of technology layered over the spiritual principles I've learned over my lifetime, starting with those instilled by my godly parents, to help lead Crossroads to continued fruitful days of ministry outreach.

Fay and I met in high school and were married at the age of 20. Since then we have worked with teenagers both as youth leaders in our church for 17 years and through coaching hockey for 20 years, all in the same community. We have traversed a lot of tough circumstances, but Dylan's death, more than any other experience, has helped us crystallize our thinking about a perfect storm that our young people are in… magnifying this epic battle that we all face, a battle of two worlds that are after our souls. Fay and I have always had a burdened heart for young people primarily because we feel so fortunate to have met Jesus at the age of 16. In my case, I was a "church brat" and I always said, "if God "got me", whatever He used would be very potent." Well, he used a local church youth group, and the dedicated volunteer leaders there who "loved me anyway." Finding God in this time of rebellion so turned things around that we have felt spared from enormous life heartache, as we learned and applied God's principles and accepted His instructions for our "provision and protection". So we have loved youth leaders who, so often, are volunteers. The Lord (and very understanding partners and family members) allowed us to take breaks from the businesses we were involved in and actually visit hundreds of churches across Canada in order to strengthen and serve youth leaders in personal ministry and encouragement. For Fay and I, these relationships and visits were some of life's richest experiences and will always be cherished memories. We love young people and our desire is to see them develop a heart for God and a heart for people as early in life as possible. In retrospect, it should not surprise us that this was excellent training ground for God's call to now lead such an influential Canadian ministry.

As I cast the vision for Crossroads' future at its 50th Anniversary Gala honoring such strong work through David Mainse and the teams that had preceded us, I asked the leaders and supporters present to embrace an expanded vision to reach all ages at all stages through every modern media platform available today. With the advent of Crossroads TV, offering multiple channels of programming available 24/7, we are now poised to minister to the nearly three billion people who can access the Internet. We have many plans to provide more content and programs to change lives and strengthen families. Surely, the Lord is expanding our territory and outreach and I live each day in humble dependence upon Him as the senior leader.

What motivates me? How can I keep up under such a demanding schedule? Obviously, my wife Fay, and my children are my heroes supporting and energizing me. Remember, I am a hockey coach and have mentored young men for years. Perhaps one of my former hockey players, Dylan, has forced me to realize, more than anything else, the aggressiveness with which we must proceed and use whatever means to make sure our kids know that they are so very precious to God. As Jesus reminded us, the souls of our kids are more valuable than owning the whole world. Let me tell you Dylan's story.

Up to this point, it was a fairly usual bus trip for a high school hockey team. Full of fun and frolic, a few bad jokes, and eager competitions for room team points.

We were about to watch, the movie, *Miracle*, about the United States men's hockey team, led by head coach Herb Brooks (Kurt Russell), who won the gold medal in the 1980 Winter Olympics, held in Lake Placid, New York. Everyone on our bus had watched the movie many times. In fact, some of the guys could even give coach Herb Brooks' famous coach's speech *verbatim*.

It was the story of an underdog USA team ending up in the gold medal game against the heavily favored Soviet team, who had won nearly every world championship and Olympic tournament since 1954. The USA team's victory over the Soviets in the gold medal round was dubbed the *"Miracle on Ice"* and in 1999 was named by Sports Illustrated, the "Top Sports Moment of the 20th Century!"

Here we were, a Canadian hockey team headed to Lake Placid to play in the American Cup High School Tournament, where the games would be played in that same Olympic complex; some of them on the very same ice surface, now called *The Herb Brooks Arena*, in which that "miracle" took place.

We needed a miracle! Our team was from Uxbridge, Ontario, a very small town of 10,000 with just one high school. Our school was returning to the Lake Placid Tournament for the second time since the school had a hockey team. In the first excursion several years earlier, both our boys and our girls teams took the gold. ("No pressure" as we say in the world of sports!)

We were clearly outclassed and had to admit to ourselves that we were the undisputed underdog. It would take a miracle to stay in for the playoff rounds, let alone win the whole tournament!

My young friend, Dylan, was our goalie. It was his last year of high school, just a month or so from his last game as a Tiger, having been a key part of our Varsity team for 3 years. For Dylan, and this group of young men, I suspect that this was one of their best hockey memories ever.

We were playing teams that were stronger than we were. Every game was a close one, where we won two and tied one of our first three division games scoring only two goals in each game. If you've experienced a points tournament, you know the drill. That tied division game meant that we had to battle for the right to go on to the finals. It was Saturday night, our fourth and final division game, and the tournament was so close at that point. We had to win or we'd go home. To make matters worse, we knew that we would have to win by a margin of 3 goals. Ending up with a win by even 2 goals would send us home.

Now you have to understand that even as a competitor who hates losing and loves winning, for us winning at hockey is still not the most important thing for us to help the young men of the Uxbridge Tigers experience. Our coaching staff are all community volunteers, with most of us from Uxbridge High School ourselves. We've been together for ten years now; a dairy farmer, an emergency nurse, our former Principal, a committed teacher coach, and my son Craig, who lobbied the school to start the team in his final year and as a result he is a first year team alumni. We do our very best to use sports to help young men learn important character traits such as respect, responsibility, courage, honesty, gratitude and optimism. In fact, each of the players carry the responsibility for one of 14 character traits throughout our season, helping the whole team live out their assigned trait in practical ways.

This is matched with our desire to help each of them become a *"whole"* hockey player... where the specific training and skills of hockey are just one of five parts. The four other areas of focus are: their physical wellbeing (sleep and nourishment), their intellectual and academic development, their relationships (with teammates, friends, family, authorities) and the importance of one's inner self (self identity, self worth, self confidence and their spiritual self).

This background is important to this story as we had just three minutes left in Saturday night's game – a seesaw battle that was still tied 0-0 at that point. You don't have to use your imagination to picture me pacing up and down the bench, with obvious concern written all over my face ... when I heard Kyle Arbour, #13 say, "Hey coach, remember the trait of *optimism!*"

Having played forty-two minutes with no goals scored, knowing we had to score three while holding them to 0, I chuckled inside as Kyle applied his appointed character trait the very way I'd asked him to – the trait of optimism and... sure enough, with just two minutes to go, big Pete Luinstra #7, sniped a rising shot that picked the upper right hand corner of the net. It was 1-0. But a mere win would not do the job. There were 50 seconds left and the face-off was in our opponent's end. Our best strategy coach, Mr. Evans, set up the plan with our Captain Tavis Smith #11 (who usually played defense) taking the face off, and big Pete coming through the circle. The play worked perfectly and Pete picked up the languishing puck and sniped that rising shot in the other top corner. 2-0.

With maximum pressure from the other team, the puck drifted into our end and even before it happened, everyone knew what was on goalie Dylan's mind ... we could tell he was going to skate out and play the puck, one of his specialties. Now I wish I could say that he passed it up and we scored the final goal ... but I can't. Dyl actually mishandled the puck right at this crucial moment and the other team's player picked it up and shot at our open net!

In a classic Dylan moment, we all watched as he dove back with a full stick extension and stopped that otherwise certain goal. He didn't stop there; he played the puck again, this time successfully up to our center and top goal scorer, Mike Ramsey #27 who, with just twenty-four seconds left, made one of his famous moves on their goalie and roofed the backhand game winner putting us into the final playoff round on Sunday morning.

All of the marks of a Tiger converged in that three minutes of hockey...three minutes and a tournament win that none of us will ever forget. Our boys went out and dominated the highest rated team in the final game with a 2-0 conclusive win. Uxbridge Tigers hockey lore says the win that day made their coach cry *real* tears. (But, of course, what happens in a hockey dressing room stays in a hockey dressing room!)

Sure enough for each of the players, this tournament, and the gold medal win, marked one of their very best hockey memories. A picture is worth more than words, so there is a picture of our team—moments after the victory—in the photo montage section of the book.

It was early in the morning on January 6th just over two years after our Lake Placid experience. I received a text message and then confirmed the terrible news. Soon the phone was buzzing with calls from other coaches. Emotions were high and there was little to say as we were stunned and speechless with the reality of the news. Word spread within our small community of the unbelievable fact that Dyl had taken his own life. He had returned home late the night before and thereafter, in the early hours of the morning, took a rope and hung himself in a small subdivision forest a few houses away from his.

Dylan had played hockey with his friends during the week. He had been at a Toronto Maple Leaf game just the night before with his girlfriend. He was due to return to his second semester classes at university the next day. All seemed normal.

Dylan's mom and dad asked if I would do the eulogy at the funeral. Here is what I said as I faced my surviving hockey team, dressed in their Tigers jerseys and hundreds in our community searching for answers, wondering why:

My friend Dylan ...

Good afternoon friends. On behalf of everyone gathered here, and those unable to be present in person today, may I say first to Jamie, Cheryl and Nicole ... and their extended family how very sorry we are for this indescribable loss. I am unable to come up with words that can adequately convey the deep sense of grief that your community feels with you.

Dylan embraced life: his family and friends were his world.

Most people who crossed paths with Dyl quickly drew similar conclusions. Dylan was incredibly unique, incredibly talented, incredibly intense, and incredibly fun. His interests and abilities spanned many worlds within and outside of our small community. Last Friday news spread quickly traversing wide networks of family, friends, musicians, teachers, churches, teammates, employers, and so many that his life has touched. Just look at the outpouring of love and support here today... you can see what I mean.

It is a privilege for me to honor Dylan this afternoon.

I would like to talk very directly to you today. I have to say that Dylan's passing at age 20, just starting the prime of life, and the way Dylan died, is the ultimate tragedy for any family, any group of friends, and indeed for any community. In honoring Dylan today, the French family has also asked that we consider, honestly, the implications of Dylan's life—and death —with a view to avoid such tragedy in the future. It is only in avoiding more tragedy that Dylan's death might accomplish some purpose.

The name Dylan, is welsh for "man of the sea", he was well named, because Dyl loved anything to do with water. He loved times at the cottage, swimming, sailing and waterskiing. He also loved visiting his cousins in Lunenberg, Nova Scotia. He used to dive down for scallops in the 53-degree Atlantic and would outlast everyone else in the frigid water.

And there is the musical Dylan. He loved music and its freedom of expression. Early on he had a vision with his band to impact society with messages conveyed through music. Many of you will know the band 'In Lights' as they recorded and played their music, once heading to eastern Canada on tour. Guys, he loved doing music with you.

Then there is the suave Dylan ... it seemed that even before the bus would stop at an arena, he would have the text address of the best looking timekeepers at the tournament ... Dyl, how did you do that? And his female friends were important in his life at a relatively young age, he was such a cool guy to be with. And Katie, our sympathies are extended to you.

There is the friend Dylan ... he had an ability to traverse many friend groups past and present, often as the life of the party. His friends knew Dylan's complex, and sometimes-conflicting qualities: intense but lighthearted, thoughtful but fun, at times so focused, yet at times so easily distracted. One of the attractive things about Dylan was his interest in deeper aspects of life, why something was unfair, or what might be done about an issue. This often made friendships with him heavy, yet meaningful, and this was indeed an intriguing aspect of Dylan the friend.

And then there was Dylan, Defender of Justice. He was always standing up for the little guy, or someone who was getting shafted. If you Google Dylan's name, you will find the first entry is his interview with the paper defending a teacher at the school. If he felt someone being attacked, he would be right there, defending. I remember him coming to our rescue as coaches at a tournament, when our team was fighting within itself in the dressing room. We were trying to explain that a lack of unity would result in certain defeat ... and in grade 10 he stood up to his older peers to defend the concept of unity ... even when as coaches, we were in the minority at that moment.

Which brings me to Dylan, straight up. A tough but refreshing part of relating to Dylan was his direct and straightforward way. He 'was who he was' and most people around him respected him for that, while at the same time running into it head on at some point in their relationship with him. In fact, he would expect me to be direct and candid in speaking with you today, without sugarcoating this very situation.

There was Dylan the competitor and teammate. Everyone would agree he was the best of teammates, one that would leave everything on the ice for his team. He was intensely competitive, he hated to lose, and he was naturally talented, able to walk in and perform with little preparation. Goalies often have unique personalities, and Dylan sure did. One didn't really know just what to say during the preparation time for a game. Sometimes he would want to fool around, and other times, often abruptly he would want solitude, to gain focus and warm up his catching hand with tennis balls off the walls in his own custom made drill. Regardless, his teammates played confidently and played well when he had their back as their goalie.

And there was Dylan, a brother. He was proud of you Nicole. He loved seeing how hard you worked at school and hockey. He was proud of your achievements. Interestingly, he was very proud of how clearly you saw things about his life, even though you often did not agree with him. In fact, while he struggled in his own choices, he was incredibly impressed at how solid your own personal standards and faith decisions had become.

And Dylan, the son. God created the teenage years as the passage between childhood to adulthood. And for Mr. and Mrs. French and Dylan, this has not been a smooth road. Having drawn a line on what was allowed or not allowed in their home (which by the way is not only their right, but their responsibility) Dylan decided to move out in grade 10. It was an anxious time, but I noticed that Cheryl always brought his equipment for him to the arena. And Jamie and Cheryl, while there's lots you would do differently (like all of us parents), Dylan loved you even through these disagreements—it's just that he didn't always show it. He knew down deep it was your love for him that was at the root of these challenges. I know he knew of your love, because he told me so.

Dylan was selected as a goalie for the Uxbridge Tigers Varsity team in grade 10. Not many grade 10's are selected because the Varsity team goes right up to second year grade 12's. This tells you something about Dyl.

And in grade 11 we were forced to cut Dylan as he rolled in to the tryouts out of shape and unprepared, assuming his strong participation in grade 10 automatically earned him a spot in grade 11. This tells you something about Dyl.

But in grade 12 Dylan was back again, intent on making the team that did not take him the year before. And he came eager, tenacious, sharp, alert, in shape and was an obvious selection for the next two years. And this tells you a lot about Dyl.

Dylan carried all 5 marks of a Tiger.

- *He was alert.*

- *He played with heart.*

- *He used his head.*

- *He was a great team player*

- *And, he loved winning so much that he hated losing.*

I first met Dylan during an interview process that we conduct with each player trying out for the team. We have a series of questions we ask and one is "what is your biggest life challenge right now." Often the answers range from poor grades to trying to come up with enough money for hockey. But in Dylan's case, he shared very honestly that he was on a search for life's meaning. He had put his life in God's hands a year earlier, but was finding it difficult to make his day-to-day choices God's way. We appreciated his openness and honesty. I explained that I had lived through the same experience as a young man in grade 10. And this created a certain bond between us.

As I speak to you today, it is almost impossible for me to believe that Dylan is not with us. That such a unique and special young man, with so much potential, so much to live for—so much to offer to our world—won't be able to fulfill his purpose—it's just beyond belief.

Jamie, Chery, Nicole, a Tiger is never forgotten. And today we are retiring Dylan's jersey # 29 out of respect for our missing player.

I must admit to being troubled with my own lack of assistance to Dylan in his time of need. You see our Tigers hockey motto is to help our players 'win at hockey and win in life'. I can't help feeling like a coach who has deeply failed my player... where we won at hockey, but not in life, and of the two, winning in life is far more important!

The way Dylan's life ended disturbs us all. And I am not

one that feels Dylan was right to choose this path. Instead, I believe that life itself is the greatest gift each of us is given. You and I have the most sacred responsibility to value our lives with a view to becoming everything we were intended to be. There is never a reason good enough to yield to life's pressures and end our life on purpose ... no matter how great those pressures become. And I urge you today never to allow yourself, ever, to think this is could possibly be the right choice for you. Slam the door shut on that option for the rest of your life. In fact, I wish I had added one more character trait called "live" and I wish I had assigned that one to Dylan.

In the last five years we have lost thirteen precious young lives from our school. These are the sons and daughters of our Uxbridge community. And trying to make sense of this especially for those in Dylan's age group has been very difficult. And so many tragic events can impact a person, and cause them to lose hope. And we cannot let this happen. You must not let this happen.

Could we take this outcome of Dylan's decision and turn it into some good? We can actually help find real purpose to his life by committing right here and now, never, ever to give up on life itself!

- This is why I dream of a community whose young men and women know the difference between right and wrong.

- This is why I dream of a community whose young men and women encourage each other to make the wisest choices.

- This is why I dream of a community whose young men and women voluntarily respond to that challenge from each other.

- That is why I dream of a community whose young men and women see the importance of following the guidance *of their parents, teachers and those trying to help them.*

Dylan's decision raises so many questions. Difficult questions. Unanswerable questions. But, those closest to Dylan feel that he was caught in an epic battle that we all face, a battle of two worlds that are after our soul.

Just like we have a physical body that you can touch and feel, and a mind, complete with a unique personality and set of emotions, we also have a spiritual dimension ... some deny its existence of course, but it is as real as our physical and emotional dimensions.

God Himself created you for a specific purpose. You are not an accident and your unique differences and abilities are designed for something only you can do. And it is finding that purpose that give us hope and optimism, even in the face of life's troubles or the unfair circumstances that are sure to come to us all.

So, you need to know that destructive forces will work life-long to distract and disrupt your quest for this ultimate life purpose for which you were created. God's original design and plan for you is one that is hopeful, purposeful and for your good. But many people, not just young people ... are looking for hope and purpose in the wrong places. And our dear friend, Dylan, got caught between these two worlds... and ultimately lost his hope for living.

No one has to get caught in between.

Dylan's love for boating made me think of an example to help us make sure Dylan's death does not continue this despair, but instead begins a whole new sense of hope within our community. A boater has no difficulty understanding the importance of an anchor when the weather gets rough. If one does not use a solid anchor, their boat could drift into a perilous situation and get lost at sea. It's the same in our lives. But not one of us have to get lost in the sea of life, because God has promised to anchor us so that not one of us will ever have to face what Dylan did.

As a final tribute to our missing friend, and to make sure that the tragedy of Dylan's death actually brings new hope, I want you to always remember a verse from the Bible found in Hebrews 6:19:

This hope [in God] is a strong and trustworthy anchor for our souls.

I need that hope in my life. Dylan needed that hope. You need and can have this hope as well. It will hold you solid and secure through the storms of life.

Friends, its time to put our anchors down.

Good bye Dyl.

Coach Don and Dylan

CHAPTER 5

Life and Death Lessons For Teachers

"Disturbing behavior is not the problem.
It is only a symptom of the problem."

Patty, grade 11 with above average grades and many friends, broke up with her boyfriend. They had gone together for two years. Patty tried talking it over with her parents, but they teased her about puppy love and said she would get over it as soon as the next guy came along.

The talk ended in a loud argument, and Patty ran into the bathroom and slammed the door. Unknown to her parents, she grabbed a bottle of prescription sleeping pills and a bottle of painkillers. Minutes later she raced from the house.

Patty drove to the other side of town, an area where the family had once lived. She bought a six-pack of colas; parked outside the grammar school she once attended, and swallowed all the pills. As she waited for the pills to take effect, she thought about her days in grammar school. Patty remembered one teacher, Mrs. Blanchard, who had been kind and friendly. She started the car and through directory assistance obtained Mrs. Blanchard's telephone number. Like many other teen suicides Patty did not want to die but she did not want to live ignored in her emotional pain. Patty made the call:

> Mrs. Blanchard, this is Patty and I've just overdosed and I am going to die. I just wanted to thank you for everything you did for me when I was in your class.

Mrs. Blanchard made Patty tell her where she was, quickly called 911 for an ambulance, and met Patty as the paramedics wheeled her into the emergency room. That teacher saved Patty's life. We need more teachers like Mrs. Blanchard. Unfortunately, some teachers regard their profession as merely a job, and they make little attempt to relate to their students on a personal level.

And other teachers see only the problems and complications of young people and give up. Some common patterns of thought are: "You can never counter the problem, so why try?" "Drugs have been here ever since I had a job, and they will always be here." "Kids are going to end up killing themselves because they are in such horrible home environments, and we can't do anything to change that."

I have traveled across the United States and to nearly every Canadian province talking in schools and in conferences with educators, teachers, principals, school administrators, and students. Some do care—and they care a whole lot. Others care, but they don't seem to know how to help. Because of their positions, teachers can do much to help. There are many "Pattys" out there, wanting to believe in an adult, wanting just one teacher to relate to.

By the way, suicidologists point to Patty, who took enough pills to kill her, and then made a call as a *cry for help*. This is common in the lives of depressed young people. They do not want to die, but they do not want to live in the state of neglect and hopelessness in which they feel they have descended. Cries for help can manifest themselves in many different ways. A depressed teen can start writing about death hoping someone will care enough to notice. In addition, suicidal young people will make flippant comments about death, "No one will ever miss me" or "I'd be better off dead than alive." The abuse of drugs and alcohol, anorexia, bulimia, violent behavior, and sexual promiscuity are cries for help. Some suicide cries are verbal, and most are non-verbal. We must notice, and we must intervene. Here are twelve tips for teachers who want to help keep kids alive.

1. Make yourself available. Do you know how many times after speaking, exhausted, anxious to get back to the hotel, a student has made a *cry for help* to me? Innumerable. And I have always stopped because I know these are serious, veiled threats and sincere pleas for someone to pay attention.

Be sensitive to your student's moods and needs. Express frequently your desire to get to know them one-on-one— but not on the basis of your desire to counsel with them. If teenagers know you care about them, you will not have to offer to listen to their problems. They will come to you because you care. Tony heard me in his high school in St. Louis, Missouri and wrote:

> Hi, the reason of this letter is because I'm a druggie and I was at DeSoto High School when you came there to talk. I've got to get some help because I think I should not live in this world anymore. I've got to have pot or some other drugs before I go to bed. Please help me. I'm crying out for Help. I may not live any more.

2. Be faithful to your students. Hold in confidence the things said in confidence. Too often when I stand before school audiences and say, "Talk to your teacher or counselor," scores of kids in an audience of one thousand snicker and laugh. To them, the last person they would ever think of going to and talking to is a teacher or a counselor. They have some good reasons for that.

Students have been betrayed in the past. If not by you, by someone else in the profession. Hurting kids went to counselors or teachers and told them about their problems. Those professionals went directly to their parents and repeated what they learned. Or they gossiped to other teachers and leaked the information to other students or to brothers and sisters. In a previous chapter I wrote that there have been times during a counseling session with a suicidal teen where I have sensed the imminent danger of the student and have felt prompted that their parents needed to know the gravity of situation immediately. *But, I always tell the young person why I am going to alert their parents.* I explain that I feel like they are in serious peril and that I am obligated to help them by notifying their parents. I only do this when I am convinced the teen might take their life. Again, I have learned how critical a situation is when a young person, depressed, has logically thought through a plan or method to kill them, and has scheduled a specific timetable of when to do it. You can't pat them on the back and let them leave your office. However, before I pick up the phone I carefully explain *why.* I don't view this as betrayal, rather a proper response to their cry for help.

On the other hand, unless it becomes a matter of life and death, it is not professionally ethical to divulge counseling information, whether or not students preface the information with the statement, "I don't want anyone to know." Joan wrote me a letter that illustrates this point:

I feel so alone and I feel like you're the only one in the whole world who I can talk to. I don't really have any close friends anymore, but recently I met this group of girls who are into all kinds of drugs. And I found myself being offered drugs: pot, speed, and I accepted. And now I'm afraid. I am afraid of getting into drugs but I'm afraid that if I say no they won't want to be friends and then I'd be back where I was before & alone. I just don't know what to do anymore. The counselor I'm going to now tells my parents everything, even if I ask her not to. I don't need someone to run to my parents every time I tell them something. So it always ends up that I don't tell her anything any more. Lately I've been Thinking about hanging myself. I don't want to but I can't go on like this anymore.

3. Move to your student's level. Find out what's going on in the world of young people. Teachers and counselors, whom they automatically stereotype as busy people, and who care little about students, too often turn off teenagers.

Some students feel teachers act as if they could not identify with teenagers who want to drink, do drugs, or have sex—activities that teens call fun today and that almost everybody does. A part of all of us wants to do the same things, and we need to face these facts. But students "know" when they approach the ultra-straight, ultra-hypocritical, and ultra-square that those teachers would never have any desire to do such things. Christy wrote me this sad letter and enclosed a poem:

I wrote this just before my last suicide attempt.
This is how I felt. I don't know if I feel this way now.
I'm just confused.
I thought there was such a thing as love
Though now I know I'm wrong.
I'll never find someone to love
Anyone like me.
So now I go and leave this world
And into a deep sleep stay.
Please do not cry or shed
Even one lonely tear.
Just look in your heart.
I will always be there.

4. Talk without giving orders. Teenagers don't want to be preached at when they have problems. They want someone to listen. Simply by listening and showing that you understand, you can help them get over many of their problems.

By listening you will help teenagers face the problems of despair, personal dilemma, drugs, alcohol, or whatever their problems may be.

It's probably a waste of time writing to you because (1) you're just too darn busy to read letters from unimportant people, (2) you have thousands of letters like this one and (3) I'm not special. For example, I'm not dying or contributing one million dollars... sorry about that. I've listened to you in person, and I've listened to your talks. And quite frankly, I like you, sir. But I wonder about things. Are you sincere? Do you speak the truth? Do you really care about people. Will I ever have the chance of hearing you speak again? Questions such as these. I'd like to say briefly that the last time I entrusted personal problems to [an adult] that very [person turned] out to be taking drugs ☺ such as cocaine! ☺ I can't tell you how terribly betrayed I felt. I pray that you are different because we teens need someone we can really trust.

Love and respect,

Kelly

5. Disseminate effective material. Avoid material written for those who have doctoral degrees and an intelligentsia vocabulary. Naturally, materials must be accurate and certain information of value, but teenagers must be able to relate to them.

Here is an unsigned letter I received from a teenage guy. His first sentence apparently refers to the lecture I gave at his school.

I thought it was dumb because people who can't handle

drugs should not try it. I can handle it. The only reason I am still alive is because of pot, skiing, and girls. But ☺ if you had people around you like me, you would do drugs, too.

6. Be alert. Look for trouble. Teachers and other school workers are usually the first professionals to encounter suicidal children and that puts them in a position to recognize the seriousness of the emotional disturbance.

Watch for telltale signs such as depression—the most frequent cause of suicide. Depression is often triggered in young people by feelings of loss. Watch for other predictable circumstances such as divorce, new transfers to school, and unstable parental job situations. Alert teachers are ready to grapple with these situations and help when students need to talk to somebody. Here is part of a letter I received from a teenager who finally went to a teacher for help. She tells of her problems and then says:

Then my sister had me over to help with her new baby and my brother-in-law molested me. . . I didn't know what to do. I just cried all night. I told my sister and they got it all straightened. It kept building up inside of me. Then one night I tried to kill myself. The next day I had to talk to someone so I went to one of the teachers an got it all straightened out.

7. Feel—and let them know you feel. Young people feel loss keenly, loss of almost anything—loss of a parent, loss of success in school, loss of self-esteem or self-respect, loss of friends, loss of a football or basketball game, loss of a familiar neighborhood, even the loss of childhood.

Try to watch closely students whom you know have experienced a definable loss—the loss of a parent through divorce or death, for instance, or the loss of the familiar because of a move. Most teenagers struggle with the loss of their security and identity as children. When this inevitable but painful loss is complicated by yet another loss, serious problems often develop.

Be especially on the alert for teens that have recently moved and are trying to fit into the school. Residential mobility is difficult on teenagers, all the more so when they have a steady boyfriend or girlfriend, athletic connectedness, and a set of established friends. In their new surroundings they want to fit in, but they're not always readily accepted. Maybe they're teased, made fun of, or just left out. They'll talk about special friends they had at their old school or about teachers they could talk to when they were upset or confused. Please don't underestimate these feelings, these losses.

8. Be especially alert to behavioral changes. Young people are action-oriented, and they often reveal their feelings through actions rather than words. Sudden changes in behavior can be warning signals.

Allan's record, for example, show high academic achievement through grade nine. Now in grade 10, he barely passes and frequently picks fights with other guys. Of course, the new subject matter may be too difficult. But watch that student closely. Allan may be trying to raise his self-esteem by punching out the next guy. Maybe he is trying to compensate in the physical area for failures in the academic or dating areas. If so, being punished will only further lower his self-esteem. Punishment is attention, but it's not the attention he needs. It does not get at what really troubles him. He may have an emotional problem at home or something serious may be going on inside Allan.

Similarly, when Barbara, who has generally been well behaved, starts to become disruptive, look beyond the symptoms. Why does she start arguments? Why has she become difficult to reason with? What has caused her hostility and lack of cooperation? Barbara may feel lousy about herself. She may feel ugly or unpopular or stupid. Perhaps she had sex with a guy and he dumped her. Maybe she feels left out or lonely. Her hostility and anger, even though lashing out, may be an expression of her desire for self-destruction. A perceptive, caring teacher may be able to help Barbara sort out her negative feelings and come to terms with the real source of her anger.

One insightful teacher said, "Disturbing behavior is not the problem. It is only a symptom of the problem." If teachers can't help teenagers like Allan and Barbara by providing some relief from their problems and their pain, these troubled teenagers may find their own relief. They may find it in drugs, sex, alcohol, or even suicide.

9. Don't become a junior psychiatrist. That's dangerous. You might open wounds you cannot close. Once you show you care, you can listen. You can probe, but don't try to solve problems by using techniques you learned from a college psychology class. Stay in your field as a teacher who wants to be a friend. Listening and caring are two unbeatable techniques you have to offer.

A middle-school student who signed himself S.O.S. wrote me a letter. He gave it to one of his teachers and asked him to pass it on. In the letter to his teacher he wrote:

> P.S. Please give it to him. My life is counting on him. If he would like to get in touch with me faster, he can ask my friend, Bob, in Mrs. Mitchell's homeroom."

In his letter to me, S.O.S. included drawings on the envelope with a note: Doomsday for some people maybe me in one week.

> I just wanted to talk to you about what you were telling us on Monday. I'm in grade eight. What I'm trying to say is that I was going to kill myself after school that day. I thought about it now. I think I will go ahead and do it. I'm scared to do it. I never took drugs before, but I think that's what I'll use to kill myself. I thought it would help. I had talked to my best friend about it. He said it wouldn't help. It would just make it worse. All I want to do is talk to you about it. But first I would get my best friend, Bob, to

talk to you to make sure it is ok for me to talk to you. I can trust him.

PS. I'll tell you why I want to kill myself.

10. Make referrals. If the school has a psychologist, social workers, and/or a counselor, take advantage of their specialized skills. This does not mean you have to back out of the picture. You can say, "You have real problems and I wish you would talk to Ms. Gannett, the school counselor. I'd still like to be available for you to talk to whenever you want. But your situation is beyond my skill."

If you show your willingness to be there, to be someone to talk to, and that you care, you are doing the best you can do. Don't attempt to function as a psychiatric professional. A parent sent the following letter to her daughter's school principal following one of my school assembly presentations:

"The tape of that young boy's suicide frightened Gail, saddened her and gave her a lot more insight into the real, horrible, and killing world of drugs. I am thankful she was scared. I am thankful she did shed tears for this boy's agony, but the thing I am most thankful for, is because of Jerry's message, she said she had never tried drugs, and she swore she never never would try them. I don't know if Gail would ever have gotten involved with drugs, but because of you and Jerry, I honestly believe that she will not be tempted to experiment – she said she will never forget the lessons taught to her Wednesday. I thank you for being the wonderful educator that you are and I thank everyone else connected with this program."

11. Contact parents. While teachers need to hold matters in confidence, there are times, like mentioned beforehand, where a teach needs to contact the parents. If you sense that a teenager is suicidal, suffering from sexual molestation, this puts a duty on you to protect and warn, and to do anything possible to prevent that student from destroying his or her life.

Communicate with the parents confidentially. You may need to say that you think their son or daughter is suicidal. If it is sexual molestation, assist the parents in notifying the law enforcement community. Remember, in most cases of molestation it is not "danger-stranger" taking advantage of a girl. Most often, it is some close friend or family member who has socialized the parents and victim beyond awareness and suspicion. Let the parents know of your concern and the reasons for it. Alert them. Occasionally a parent will resent it, particularly if they are living in denial, but most are appreciative. Working together, you and the parents can find a remedy.

12. Ask help from other teachers. Seek insight and help from other teachers who know the student. If those teachers confirm what you have observed—for example, that Barbara has suddenly become disruptive—it confirms your feelings. You know you are on to something.

Of course, what I am saying assumes that teachers have classes of manageable size. Otherwise, you are not likely to be able to provide individual attention that enables a troubled child to be spotted. In offering these tips, I am not trying to place guilt on teachers for not doing more. After a suicide occurs in a school or community, there is more than enough guilt to go around. You can even help there. Students will ask each other and you, "Why did we ignore Allan?" "Why were we so mean to him?" You and other teachers will ask yourselves questions such as, "Why didn't I notice he was troubled?" "Was it my fault—because I failed him on his last exam?"

You can help these people. They don't need toothy smiles and phony assurances of, "Don't worry—it wasn't your fault." Those words mean nothing. They will need someone to listen and to hear them speak of their own sense of failure. And, if they failed, help them to accept it. It may help if you analyze what went on, explain its complexity, and provide the guidance that will allow them to come to terms with their guilt, their sadness, and their fear.

An editorial addressed to teachers, principals, and school officials appeared in *USA Today* after a suicide in public high school:

> "The principal should not wait. By the time he hears the details, the rest of the school will have heard the details, too, in 40 different versions.
>
> "The principal must notify the parents. Then, he should call a school wide assembly and explain as much as he knows. If students are let out without explanations, they will make up their own.
>
> "He should designate staff students can turn to. He should have mental health professionals there to answer questions. Ideally, teachers would already have information about suicide and depression.
>
> "That evening, he should hold a community meeting for all parents and students. This will give the parents information. It will let the teenagers have a forum for their concerns and a place to go rather than hanging out and escalating the hysteria these situations often provoke.
>
> "The mental health professionals should be in school all day, every day, for the next three weeks. They should speak to all close friends and classmates of the boy who committed suicide. They should target and support any who have recently experienced a loss, particularly one by death.
>
> "The principal should not call off school so everyone can attend the funeral. Kids need to express their grief; they do not need to romanticize a mistake.
>
> "A boy tragically made the wrong choice. This calls for sorrow, not honor. We should not make a youngster

who made a poor choice into a hero. Instead, we should applaud the wisdom of those who choose to start psychotherapy and take constructive actions to deal with their concerns."[17]

Some leaders within the faith community are reticent to include or recommend the utilization of professionals within the mental health community. These enthusiasts have something of a *"sola scriptura"* (by Scripture alone) conviction that does not include mental health professionals in the equation of prevention and post-trauma of suicide and other psychiatric disorders. This is regrettable because mental illness does exist. In my career I meet psychiatrists, psychologists, sociologists, mental health therapists, and counselors who have insightful expertise and are extremely effective. Yes, there are some professionals from this field who have a worldview which excludes Scripture and faith in Jesus Christ. And that is unfortunate.

I must also say it is a mistake of leaders within the mental health community to exclude the faith community leaders. The two must work together. Spiritual leaders bring great comfort, and biblical direction to the acute problems of depression and suicide. The proclamation and study of theology, and its application in the lives of people, has transformed untold millions of people, myself included, who at one time were suicidal or entrenched in behaviors that were addictive and unhealthy. Additionally, academics must recognize the spiritual component to the wholeness and health of young people and adults: physically, mentally, emotionally, and spiritually. I am aware we cannot "preach" in a public school. But to eliminate seasoned, reputable, theologically trained pastors from the prevention and healing process of youth suicide is a critical error and mistake. Both mental health and clergy leaders must work together to curb this epidemic.

In our next chapter we learn how some young people and adults are actually predisposed to die by suicide. It is essential that we understand these predispositions and know how to respond. Read on for some life-saving information.

CHAPTER 6

Predispositions To Suicide

*Experts refer to the trigger mechanism, some negative
experience that is the final impetus to commit suicide.*

Don't worry about me because I've been talking to God for over a year now, and I am going to heaven where I will be happy. God doesn't like me coming home early, but he doesn't like the devil beating the hell out of my mind every day either. I'm sorry, but the devil has my mind and I must escape him before I do something wrong. Be happy for me, not upset, for I have left the devil now, and he can reach me no longer. I feel relief now. Wish me luck and happiness in my new life.

With these confused, fateful words, Gary ended his life. The pressure was simply too much. It is hard for some adults to understand the stresses that can build up in a teenager's mind. The burden of these stresses is like an overinflated balloon ready to explode into a thousand pieces.

Teenagers in North America are subjected to severe pressure in their peer relationships. And when things go wrong, the pressure can be just too much to bear. For many it is a shattering experience. I know because I have seen the broken pieces. I've talked with teens that have been so hurt they want to run away, be loners, or end it all.

"There is no pressure like peer pressure." That is what an

exasperated grade ten student named Cindy told me as she poured out the story of her troubled life. Cindy, like many teenagers I have counseled, wants to fit in but does not like the high price of conformity. She wants to be a part of the group, but she wonders how far she must go. "I really want my friends to like me, but I want to be my own person, too," she says, implying a choice of one or the other.

There are several ways in which teenagers are broken, and each one indicates a need for caution and concern. Experts refer to the *trigger mechanism*, some negative experience that is the final impetus to commit suicide. The trigger mechanism is a severe disappointment that finally pushes a person over the edge to die by suicide. As you read these words, many young people in North America are on the verge of death. They are barely hanging on. What will be the trigger mechanism in their lives?

Aaron Temkin Beck, M.D. is the father of Cognitive Therapy, having created and refined cognitive therapy over the course of his research and clinical career. He has published more than 550 scholarly articles and 18 books and has developed widely used assessment scales. He has received many prestigious awards including the 2006 Albert Lasker Clinical Medical Research Award for developing cognitive therapy, which fundamentally changed the way that psychopathology is viewed and its treatment is conducted. He has been listed as one of the "Ten individuals who shaped the face of American Psychiatry" and one of the five most influential psychotherapists of all time. Dr. Beck is an emeritus professor in the Department of Psychiatry at the University of Pennsylvania School of Medicine, and was asked what kind of person dies by suicide. "People who have a negative image of their lives. The critical factor is a sense of hopelessness that is characteristic of people who may have gone through severe stress such as disappointment in their careers or a breakup of a relationship. They exaggerate their problem or its consequences.[18] When Dr. Beck was asked if a suicidal tendency is a family trait, he responded, "The idea may seem silly, but people do inherit the temperament that, when combined with other factors, could lead to suicide. We know this from a study of adopted children in Denmark who were reared apart from their biological parents. Among 57 adoptees that committed suicide, there were 12 suicides among all their biological relatives. A control group of 57 nonsuicidal adoptees had only two suicides among relatives."[19]

Broken dreams. People generally tend to be idealistic about relationships when they first start out. How many people, for example, actually expect on their wedding day that they will someday be divorced from their mate? But marriages end up that way nearly 50 percent of the time in our society. One reason this happens is that people assume that they will always get along, that the relationship will just naturally get better. But relationships don't get better unless people work at them. Right relationships have been built carefully and consistently.

A teenager is the most idealistic of all human beings about friendship and romance. A teenager holds the expectation that everything will always be great, that his or her relationship will always be close. But communication breaks down, all is not great, and the closeness is lost. This situation can be traumatic, especially when a best friend is no longer, some teenagers become so despondent they consider suicide.

I encourage teenagers not to give up when friendships go through rough waters. Persons who are truly friends will be willing to work things out—and persons who stubbornly refuse to try and readily reject the relationships cannot be trusted to be there in good *and* bad times. Teens are better off without "friends" like that. No such broken relationships are worth the price of life.

Broken romances. High on the list of factors that prompt

suicide attempts among young people are broken romances. These romance-oriented suicides are some of the saddest, most heart-breaking stories I have ever heard. So many teenagers feel that when the relationship fails, so does their opportunity for fulfilled lives. When the feelings for others are strong, and when the bonds suddenly are broken, utter hopelessness can set it. This is a dangerous time.

I spoke in an Oklahoma City high school where some of the young people were used in the filming *Silence of the Heart*. This film was a gripping movie that told the unforgettable story of two young lovers who took the death plunge together. I will forever remember the feedback I received from students in that school following my lecture. To adults, the idea of killing oneself for love seemed, in most cases, foolish. However, to young people it makes sense and is real, very real. For females, who are dumped after committing sexually, coping without their "eternal" love is, for many, the hurdle too far to cross. Males as well as females may feel that absolutely *no one* will ever find the void of that perfect guy or gal.

An attractive eighteen-year-old girl from the Midwest checked into a run down New York City hotel. She had been in the room less than an hour when she phoned the night clerk and implored, "Please get me a doctor right away. Hurry!" When the physician arrived, he found her in bed, moaning and clutching an empty pill bottle of barbiturates. He had her rushed to a hospital to have her stomach pumped.

During a brief span of consciousness, the girl said that her boyfriend had jilted her. Her final words, recalled by the doctor, were, "They will all be sorry when I am dead. But if only I could have talked to somebody like you before … maybe I would not have done this."

I know I am not going to win a popularity contest with the following statement but I don't care. I am not for serious, teenage romantic relationships. In too many cases I have seen them backfire. High school is a time to have fun, set the footprints for a successful academic career, and get to know various people by not dating only one person. The real agitation is how many parents I see, that both directly and indirectly, who encourage and sometimes coax their sons and daughters to have a steady girlfriend or boy friend. You would think the parents were dating. Too me it is rather sickening. Parents, in some kind of strange way, live out their fantasies by orchestrating their teenagers' romantic lives as if they were some kind of puppet. I have never met a person who after getting married said they were glad they engaged sexually with one or more people while in high school. The emotional maturity level of a teenager is not ready for a nearly engaged, high school romance. The catastrophic numbers of teen abortions annually and girls pregnant while in high school remind us that teenagers are not the sexual wizards they think they are. Most young people don't know the scientific facts of reproduction, hence, the disproportionate number of girls unexpectedly pregnant. My message to parents is discourage high school romance. Let your son or daughter develop mentally, physically, emotionally, and spiritually during these formative years. Studies have revealed that the older a person is and the more educated the longer the marriage will last. I am aware there are probably a few exceptions to this advice. But, in most cases, I have seen high-powered, high school romance backfire. Later, I will tell you how the hyper-sexualized culture is causing our kids to become too close, too soon with devastating consequences in our chapter, Sex & Suicide. Whatever happened to teenagers enjoying life, family, sports, and not taking on adult-sized emotional baggage? Do you know what is antidotal to premature romance in a young person's life? A strong family certainly is. A dad who bonds with his daughter, talks to her regularly, helps her plan her future by discovering her talents, abilities, and gifts. A mother who connects with her son teaching him how to respect and be kind to the opposite sex passes on a priceless gift. A mom who praises her son for his strengths and helps him be determined to overcome his weaknesses. As I have said before, the role of parents is inestimable.

Suicide not only expresses hopelessness and helplessness, but it also is used to strike back at parents, who broke up the romance, at the other person for leaving school, and at teachers for being insensitive and for not caring.

To understand the revenge principle in a romance-oriented suicide, we need to think more about the nature of romance. The first sexual encounter for anyone is the one that is always remembered. When I stand up in front of a group of teenagers and ask, "How many remember the first time you had sex with anyone?" everybody who has had sex has instant recall. People may not remember the tenth time or the twentieth time, but they remember the first time. They remember who and where, and many remember the clothes they *were* wearing.

Jerry,

At age 14 I lost my virginity. Not out of peer pressure but out of ignorance. I was naïve and never knew or wondered what was right or wrong. Now I do, but it's too late. I had sex with seven different guys. Two of them were virgins. I feel bad now that I invaded their virginity. One of them is my present boyfriend. We have had sex 21 times. Almost half the time we've used a condom. I need some advice.

Lindsay

Some young people are striking back and some are saying, "It is all over for me now." For young men, the risks seem even greater, at least statistically. Psychologists theorize that males often experience more intently than females the feeling of being rejected. Both sexes feel rejection, of course, but teenage guys especially do. Incidentally, the threat of a drastic response is greater if the relationship has gone on for a long period of time.

The teenager years are a time of adaptation, so I counsel against getting so identified with another person that the teen does not know who they are and cannot function without their love interest.

Broken ideals. Perhaps the most common of broken ideals is the loss of virginity. When it happens most teenagers (even if they will not admit it) feel the deep ache within of having given up forever something very precious *at the wrong time.* Having a baby is great, but not when you are not married and still in high school. It is interesting to me that the Bible discusses how sexual promiscuity is a sin against our own body. How? Unlike coughing or sneezing, this physical act involves the whole person—mentally, emotionally, and spiritually. Our self-worth and self-respect is directly linked to our sexuality. Ask any prostitute if what I am saying is true.

Obviously, I believe strongly in the rightness of reserving oneself sexually for one's life partner in marriage of the opposite sex. I do not hesitate to take this stand. But I realize that many teenagers who hear me speak and read my writings have already given up their virginity. I don't condemn them, but I do encourage them: Don't think that having given it up you have to keep *giving in.*

This is an important issue to me because many teenagers have told me they wanted (or actually tried) to commit suicide after they became involved sexually. It is, unquestionably, a predisposition that can have adverse consequences.

Broken expectations. When a friend is unfaithful it hurts. When desires—perhaps for something really big and important—don't materialize, it hurts. When carefully laid plans fail miserably, it hurts. And the hurt can be so overpowering that one of these things can lead to suicidal thoughts and actions.

It is important not to bank on something so strongly that if it does not work out, life is not worth living. One young man told me that when he did not get the scholarship he was sure he was going to be granted, it seemed as if his world had come to an end. He considered suicide. Fortunately, he realized soon those things were not that bad. He accepted his situation, eliminated the super negative thoughts, and took another direction. Today, he is glad it all happened.

There is nothing wrong with great expectations, but there is danger when we turn our expectations into immovable objects.

Broken hearts. The most crushing blow of all is the death of a friend. Whether that death is by suicide or accident or natural causes does not really matter. A death is a death. It disturbs, it defeats, and it discourages. And as I have mentioned previously, it can provoke deadly temptations—suicidal ideation.

How tragic that one person's death should lead to another, but it happens frequently. The reasons vary, and the questions are troubling: How can I live without her? Why should I go on if he's not here? Does life have meaning anymore? Why not join him/her now?

This brings up the whole issue of celebrity deaths and their impact. In our society, movie stars, rock stars, and other celebrities become in the mind of their fans just like personal friends. It is a strange, curious reality, but it is true. I have a few friends whose names are household words. They tell me that people regularly come up to them and carry on a conversation as if they have been lifelong friends!

Some teenagers who idolize celebrities to the point they feel personally attached to them cannot handle the death of their idol. When John Lennon was killed, numerous Beatle fans around the world committed suicide. The same thing happened in the wake of other deaths: Heath Ledger, John

Belushi, Marilyn Monroe, Janis Joplin, to name a few. It happens in other countries, too.

The whole "celebrity culture" is rather odd to me. Maybe it is because I have met many celebrities throughout my career. The acting genre, in particular, is something of a mystery to me. Actors recite lines, imitate emotions, and depend upon spin-doctors to sell them to the public. Some actors have artificial, arranged marriages to help box office gross. Many of them struggle with significant addictions due their abnormal lifestyle—who wouldn't? I don't mean to be unkind—most are uneducated. And what does the media do to the general public—nearly deify them. Media celebrates their sometimes-bizarre lifestyles. It is no secret that a prime target audience of the lifestyles of rock stars and celebrities are tweens and teens. Through the miracle of modern media, with its multiple platforms of delivery 24/7, kids are bombarded virtually every hour of the day with images of irresponsible sex, drugs and alcohol, abuse, violent and bullying behavior, disregard for core values, and violators with the law. Often, the poor choices and bad behaviors of celebrities are glamorized and sensationalized, while their consequences are ignored and negated. It is all such a myth, but the masses drink the Kool-Aid and it is regrettable.

And then there are the rock stars. One study, which charted the lives of 1,050 American and European music artists between 1965 and 2005, has found they are more than twice as likely to die young than the general population. One hundred "stars" died during the study. The average age of death for American rock stars was 42, and Europeans a mere 35! "Lead researcher Professor Mark Bellis called in the report for public health policy aimed at 'preventing music icons promoting health-damaging behavior among their emulators and fans,' " the BBC reported.[20] I scrolled down the list of notable musicians dead and found all too frequently under cause of death: suicide, drug overdose, heart attack, alcohol overdose, and car accidents. Jimi Hendrix died after taking a cocktail of wine and nine sleeping pills; Doors front man Jim Morrison died of suspected heroin overdose; and Nirvana's Kurt Cobain died from a self-inflicted gunshot wound to the head. Amy Winehouse died of alcohol poisoning. Amy shot to fame with songs including, "Rehab," in which she summed up her view on seeking treatment with the chorus "no, no, no." All were age 27 when they died! US stars Jerry Garcia of the Grateful Dead, Carl Wilson of the Beach Boys and Johnny Ramone of the Ramones all died in their 50s. The professor of the study suggested that the high rate of death among older American musicians could be related to the continent's greater appetite for reunion tours, exposing the artists for more years to an unhealthy "rock'n'roll" lifestyle. "Hope I die before I get old," sung by The Who is epitaph of far too many musicians. Neil Young belted out, "It's better to burn out than to fade away." Media ignores these facts and now rockers are a part of the culture elite. Bono attends G8 Summits. Sir Mick Jagger and Sir Elton John were knighted by the Queen II. Ozzy Osbourne played Paranoid at the Queen's Golden Jubilee. Candidates for president and prime ministers are interviewed on the music video networks.

There are multiple predispositions to suicide. It is important that we know them and we are ready to graciously intervene when we see their influence prodding a teenager to consider suicide. Disappointments in life will come. My dad use to tell me, "Grit your teeth." Parents and grandparents, most of whom have experienced much more difficult circumstances in life need to teach and instill a mental toughness in their children and grandchildren by borrowing from the life lessons they have learned and passing them on to the next generation.

In our next chapter, "How to Rescue a Friend," we learn the all important steps of intervention in a person's life who is depressed and suicidal. By the discovery of these principles we can help save lives. Take particular note of the recommended action steps—they might just rescue your son or daughter or a friend who is depending upon your discernment to help them in their difficult moment of suicidal inclination.

CHAPTER 7

How To Rescue Your Friend

"Looking back, I was not there when he needed me."

W hat if I told you one of my early pastors killed himself? A man you would have never expected to die by suicide. He was a brilliant, gifted teacher and speaker, and had friends all over America. I can remember listening to his tremendous messages. When I was in the early years of my career, he and his wife befriended my wife, Cristie, and me. We developed a custom of picking a nice restaurant —taking turns at hosting one another for a delicious meal and spending hours talking. I can vividly remember those wonderful nights of fellowship, as we would stay for hours opening our hearts with one another and sharing the progress both of us were making. Some nights we dined until the restaurant was ready to turn out the lights forcing us to go home. His wife was a dear lady who was rather quiet. When she did interject a thought it was always caring and reflected her kind heart. Over a period of months, both Cristie and I noticed he was a bit sharp with his wife. It was not uncommon that he would cut her off mid-sentence or correct something she had said. To us, it came across in a demeaning manner. It was a little embarrassing, and we felt bad for her. In a sense, he treated her more like she was his child than his wife.

I held a number of conferences in his church that attracted thousands of people. I remember the many nights we would entertain some of the most celebrated communicators in America together. He was great fun and his intellect revealed he had great opinions and ideas on a myriad of subjects. I remember one night when I was going through a stressful time he called and gave me great comfort and encouragement. After a long career in one city, he received an invitation to become pastor of one of the largest churches in America. After careful consideration, he accepted. The next time we were together was one Sunday morning when I spoke for him in the auditorium of his new church that seated nearly 4,000. I can remember, as if it was yesterday, he leaned over and whispered in my ear, "Jerry, do you see why I took this church?" I didn't have the heart to respond and tell him what I was really thinking. The church seemed something of an antique to me, stuck in the past.

In his new position he became very egocentric. Frequently, he would boast to me about how much the church was paying him, his interest-free $100,000 line-of-credit, should he need it at any time. On the way home, Cristie and I commented to one another that he seemed to have changed. We remembered back to those early dinners when he shed tears and opened his heart to us about both the joys and regrets of ministry. That was the man we fell in love with. Candidly, I did not care if he pastored a little or large church. I was simply committed to him as a friend.

On a trip to a resort in an anonymous city, I received an emergency call from my friend. He told me he was resigning the following Sunday and then asked me if I would begin a new ministry with him. "Hold on," I said. "What is going on?" His son later told me that for years he had an extramarital affair with the wife of a close friend. Finally, it all caught up with him. We were so sad to hear what had happened and cordially declined a joint opportunity to work together.

My pastor friend ended up pursuing a business career in a city near where my wife was raised. Consequently, it afforded me the opportunity to keep in touch with him as we visited Cristie's parents. Several times we would go to lunch. He would often say, "I am making so much money now. It is great! I had no idea how much pressure I was under as a pastor." As he would boast, I wanted to say to him, "I don't care if you make a lot of money or a little, you are my friend, and I am always going to be your friend."

Looking back, I was not there when he needed me. A business associate left him in a precarious situation. One day in desperation, he drove to a cemetery and took a gun to his head. After struggling for several minutes, he finally died. His suicide sent shock waves across the nation. I felt so bad. Cristie and I have wept several times together asking ourselves, "Why didn't we see it coming? Why didn't we ask him if he was depressed?" Simply, "Why didn't we take more of an interest in his life?" I have wondered why he didn't call me, and tell me the problems he had found himself in. We both knew enough people that we could have put our heads together and remedied any burden. In retrospect, the tragedy of his life motivates me to tell you to be on the lookout when your friend is hurting. Take time to listen. You don't want to carry a memory, like I have, the rest of your life. Let me tell you how to rescue your friend or family member, should they be struggling like my friend was.

   1. Read the signals. Take an interest. When a friend or family member is exhibiting behavior that is dangerous and reflective of depression, make yourself more available and interested than ever. People cocooned in problems really feel like no one cares. Through this book we keep hearing the words *hopelessness* and *helplessness*. In a sense, the suicidal person feels helpless to change their deep depression. A loving friend or family member can make all the difference. It requires you to read the signals. It will require you to slow your life down long enough to care, and care enough to confront.

Dee said, "I am alive today because my best friend would not leave me alone. I was going downhill, and I kept telling her to bug off, and she kept saying things like, 'Real friends don't leave when their friends are in trouble.' I really did not want her to leave, but I didn't think anyone cared for me."

What if you don't know for sure that there is a life-threatening problem lurking inside your friend? Don't take chances! One expert counseled: "Even if you're not completely sure about the seriousness of the depression in yourself or a friend, it is better to take the necessary steps and find out you were wrong than to say nothing and find out you were right."[21]

2. Be a detective. I am not suggesting that you stalk your friend or steal a glance at their personal diary. But, I am saying to be on the lookout for problems or potential problems. The best way to accomplish this is by encouraging your friend to talk whenever you sense something wrong.

What can you ask? If your friend or son/daughter has not seemed well lately, ask something like, "You don't seem like yourself. Is there anything you would like to talk about?" If they say yes, and tell you about negative feelings and thoughts, do not hesitate to ask if these include thoughts of suicide. "When in doubt, check it out. If you are suspicious, ask the person directly," says family counselor Cynthia Taylor.[22]

If your friend or child admits to thinking about suicide, your next step is to ask, "Do you have a plan?" If the answer is affirmative, get the details. The more specific the details, the more serious the situation. More about this in a minute.

Being a good detective demands knowledge of the suicidal warning signs. Review chapter two, "Warning Signs,"

Jerry, when he was struggling with
drugs and suicidal thoughts.

Dylan will forever motivate me to lead the Crossroads
ministry to reach young people and parents for Christ.
- *Don Simmonds*

One of my greatest memories—the victory of Uxbridge
Tigers Hockey Team (Dylan is pictured in the centre).
- *Don Simmonds*

The divorce of his parents negatively impacted Kurt Cobain,
icon to a generation, who died by suicide.

British original musical genius, Amy Winehouse, 27, drank herself to death.

Jerry has spoken in hundreds of cities throughout North America and the world.

Aaron Stoufer, fifteen-year-old son of Dennis and Barbara Stoufer, killed himself with a .22 Magnum in 1985.*

Jerry's *Life School Assembly* challenges young people to avoid the dangers of drug and alcohol abuse. Jerry has been speaking to young people since 1979.

The Crossroads ministry is making an eternal difference in the lives of needy people, receiving thousands of calls on their toll-free prayer phone lines, and preventing potential suicides.

The Simmonds Family.
From Left: Don, April, Fay, Craig, Shauna, and Brett.

Dr. Jerry and Dr. Cristie Jo Johnston
both completed their doctoral degrees
at Acadia University Divinity College
in Wolfville, Nova Scotia.

periodically.

> **3. Listen carefully.** Your suicidal friend must know that
> someone is truly willing to listen. Chances are your
> friend will feel that no one at home is tuned in, so you
> have to show that you are. An insightful report in the
> *FBI Law Enforcement* Bulletin said:

> "Many suicidal young people have the inability or lack of
> opportunity to express their unhappiness, frustration,
> or failure. They find that their efforts to express their
> feelings are either totally unacceptable to their parents,
> ignored, or met by defensive hostility. This response
> then drives the child into further isolation, reinforcing
> the belief of something being terribly wrong." [23]

In Omaha, Nebraska, where five students in the same
high school attempted suicide in less than two weeks (three
died by suicide), other teenagers became concerned and got
involved. A network of listeners was organized to avert more
tragedy. In Plano, Texas, which experienced eleven teenage
suicides in just sixteen months, students set up BIONIC
(Believe It or Not I Care) and SWAT (Students Working All
Together). Through these organizations, they befriended
newly transferred or depressed classmates. Adults created a
twenty-four-hour hotline. The payoff: Teen suicides slowed
and clusters virtually ceased.

As you listen, remember that your son/daughter or friend
may be pointed or very vague. "Verbally, teenagers make
direct references to killing themselves by asking, 'What would
you do if I were to kill myself?' Indirectly, they might say,
'Everyone will be better off without me,' or 'You won't have to
worry about me much longer.' Any reference to dying must be
taken seriously."

> **4. Say the right things.** Remember that asking a person
> about suicide will not plant the idea in their mind. In
> fact, it says, "I've been paying attention to you, and I see

something's wrong." One author explains:

"It is not unusual for teenagers to respond, 'No. Are you crazy?' It is their way of protecting themselves from the possibility of being rejected, ridiculed, or treated as if they are crazy. Never settle for the first 'no.' Pursue it with words of understanding such as, 'Look, with everything happening in your life (list the incidents) and with the way you have been feeling, it is normal to feel like ending it all. It's not crazy. So, have you thought about it?' This shows you are serious, care, understand, and are free to talk about it. If they have been thinking about it, they are likely to tell after this. If they are are not suicidal, they will still respect the caring and concern and be more liable to come for help when in trouble."[24]

Here are some right things to say to a son/daughter or friend you think might be entertaining a suicidal ideation:

- "I didn't know how serious things have become. Let's talk about it."

- "It sounds like you are feeling totally hopeless. I understand how you can feel like this. Have you told anyone else? We have to talk to someone about this."

- "I don't want you to do anything to hurt yourself. I don't know how we can change the feeling, but I know there are people who can help."

- "I can't watch you twenty-four hours a day. If you want to, you will find a way, but I do not want you to, and I will do anything to keep you from killing yourself."

- "I want to hear everything that has been happening. I have time." (Be sure you do, and be willing to drop everything if you don't.)

- "Abusing drugs and alcohol like you are doing shows

there must be some inner pain you are trying to medicate. Is everything okay? Will you let me help you and get help?"

Now, it is equally important, too, to know what *not* to say. Here are a few statements to bear in mind:

- "You will get over it. Things will be better tomorrow." (Things may be better tomorrow, and making this kind of promise may make you part of the problem rather than the solution.)

- "You have your whole life ahead of you." (The suicidal person is usually convinced that 'whole life ahead' is bleak and not worth living. This might be a statement of demotivation to make a person actually think about suicide. In essence, it says, "Do you know how miserable you are feeling right now? Well let me encourage you by reminding you that you are going to feel this way the rest of your life!" Weigh your words.)

- "You don't really feel that way." (Yes, the suicidal person does feel that way. Don't allow your pride or ignorance to be showcased in the presence of someone else's emotional pain.)

- "You would never do it." (How do you know? That is almost like saying, "I dare you to try." Over 50,000 teenagers in the United States and over 2,000 teenagers in Canada completed suicide in just the past ten years!)

So, the bottom line is: Don't criticize, judge, ridicule, minimize, expose your ignorance and insensitivity, or promise anything you can't deliver.

5. *Take action*. A suicidal threat is not like the alarm on your clock radio. You can't push a snooze button and wait a while longer before you do something. I know a number of parents that knew they needed to intervene in their child's life and they waited. These parents knew down deep their son or daughter was in trouble, but they did not muster the fortitude to do what was needed to be done in time. Please don't join their company. When there is clear suicidal inclination exhibited and expressed, immediate action is called for.

- Tell your son/daughter or friend about the resources for help. Take a look in the back of this book – one of the most effective Suicide hotlines is 1-800-273-TALK (8255). There is probably a local suicide hotline in your area. Remember, the Crossroads ministry toll-free prayer lines are available 24/7 where caring people are ready to pray with you or the person whom you are concerned at 1-866-273-4444. In a few moments you will read how this essential call center has been used of God to rescue precious people in their neediest moments in life. Friends are standing by right now to take your call. Don't be hesitant and if you have a child or friend in need help make the call with them.

- It is best that your friend make the decision to seek professional help but be willing to help make the arrangements and go along to lend your support. I have been asked to lead interventions on a people when the whole family felt inadequate. These are very difficult situations. In one situation, a young lady who had been a model, descended in the depths of drug and alcohol abuse. Her desperate family asked for my help but cautioned me that she could be volatile. Candy was shocked when I entered their home and told her we loved her so much we were not going to stand back and let her die. Hours later, we checked Candy into a reputable facility to help her get back on the road to recovery. She is alive today. Generally, these surprise intervention sessions need someone leading them who have experience. But not always. When every family member has solidarity and conviction that a brother or sister, Mom or Dad is dying, and will not stand by and let it happen, that's generally all it takes. If you are a parent, it is your responsibility to intervene when your son or daughter is suicidal or out of control. Don't take the easy way out. I am aware this is a highly stressful situation. It is far less stressful than living the rest of your life with the knowledge your child took their life.

- If a specific suicide plan has been revealed, be prepared to remove the instruments of the method if possible. I want to caution parents about easy access to guns in the home. If your son or daughter is suicidal, those weapons should be under lock and key. We have too many weapons and too easy access for firearms in the U.S. Remember, the number one method of suicide is the use of firearms.

- Establish a binding agreement with your son/daughter or friend with yourself. Cynthia Taylor suggested: "Ask for a verbal contract with you that he or she will contact you or another designated person if he or she has thoughts about suicide or an inclination to complete suicide."[25] You may want to go one step further and have a written agreement with your son or daughter to the same effect. I would rather be safe than sorry.

- Pray before, with, after, and during your encounter with a suicidal friend or child.

- If your child or friend refuses to get help, contact someone with expertise and ask for his or her advice and direction in the situation. Crisis intervention counselors will tell you the person down deep wants someone to know who can bring aide, even when denying it. If you have made a promise of secrecy, break it for the sake of the person's life. Keeping a friend is more important than keeping your word when it is the brink of life or death.

If you fail to act when a friend is in grave danger, and your friend completes suicide, you will be haunted for years by the ghost of guilt. Don't let that happen. Sometimes I am overwhelmed by what teenagers tell me they are going through. They open up to me, I suppose, because in many cases I am the first person they have heard address the problems plaguing their heart. I tell teenagers everywhere, listen to your friends—some of them are in real danger and you don't know it. Let me share a letter I received from Bridgette in Colorado:

I have been really having a lot of problems... Over the summer a lot of my friends who I looked up to turned to drugs and drinking. Right now I am caught in the middle of a lot of things. One girl tried to commit suicide and is now paralyzed. And another girl who I don't even know wants to melt my face in. She doesn't use her fists. She uses guns and knives ... but that bothers me, well, not a lot. But I have been thinking about getting on drugs again. That really scares me, but I have really been thinking about it ... Well, right now I am really thinking about suicide. I have cut my wrists a couple of times. But so far I haven't found a foolproof plan. Right now I don't think I have the courage. But with each passing day I get a little more. I see a real problem coming. I am reaching out to you. Please help.

Remember I told you how the dynamic ministry Crossroads (www.crossroads.ca) based in Burlington, Ontario, Canada with a worldwide outreach has caring toll free prayer lines dedicated to take your calls day and night at 1-866-273-4444. Many of these people have watched Crossroads flagship TV show, *100 Huntley Street*, on television and God touched their hearts. I want you to know that caring people are standing by right now to help you to discover life and fulfillment. Our ministry prayer partners have been successful in their mission. Read these following stories... there is hope for you. You are only one phone call away. Call us today, write the number down for you or a friend, 1-866-273-4444.

William—Ontario (Desperation/Loneliness/Abandonment)

William had a spinal injury seven years ago as a result of a car accident. Unfortunately, his wife couldn't deal with his injury and left him. He lives alone in his own home and called in response to the program and number on the screen. Through many tears he shared with our Prayer Partner that "I don't know how to pray and I've never been to church." Our Prayer Partner led William to the Lord! In the Follow-up call he shared that he "knew he had to do something!" When we told him about a caring church in his community and that he would receive a call from the Pastor, he was overjoyed! Follow-up has now begun on the local church level to help William in his need and bring a caring church family around him. This is what makes the ministry of Crossroads so practical and far reaching.

Nicky—Alberta (Disillusionment)

Nicky comes from a Hindu family who practice their religion, but she feels guilty because she has opened her life to Jesus, yet she knows He is the only answer. Nicky had gone to a psychic who told her someone had put a curse on her autistic child and this has caused problems in her marriage. In watching *100 Huntley Street* Nicky knew she had to call the Prayer Line and receive His help. Scripture was shared and a church recommended for her to connect with. Nicky was so grateful for the spiritual help and really wants to follow Jesus, though she recognizes it may not be easy.

Don—New Brunswick (Wandering)

Don was raised in the church but wandered away. His common-law wife came to the Lord and began to share with him his need for Jesus. After watching 100 Huntley Street, Don knew he needed to call the Prayer Line and give his life to Jesus. As we talked, Don really evidenced a desire for the Lord and he was encouraged to begin reading the Bible and allow Jesus to speak to him through it everyday. In a follow-up call he expressed such appreciation for the care we were showing to him in his desire to really serve Jesus.

Alka—British Columbia (Brokenness)

Alka had an arranged marriage in India only to discover her husband was a pimp! Because she left him her family has abandoned her, and she feels so alone. Alka contacted a secular Help Line who gave her our Prayer Line number! When she called, one of our female Prayer Partners compassionately and tenderly led her to discover the love that Jesus Christ has for her. In the follow-up call we were able to take time to share God's Word with her and explain how the grace of Jesus Christ is able to take what Satan has meant for evil and turn it for good (Genesis 50:20). Alka was so deeply grateful and now has hope in her life!

Lorna Lee—Ontario (Loneliness/addictions)

Lorna Lee grew up with no Christian background in her life and said she has alienated so many people from her by the terrible things she has said to them. Lorna Lee wondered how she could possibly receive forgiveness? We spoke of forgiveness through Jesus Christ's death on the cross, sharing what the Bible says about God's love for her and His desire to give her a new beginning. Also spoke to her about the power of our words (Proverbs 18:21). Spoke life to Lorna Lee and God's purpose for her future, because He is a redeemer. Connected Lorna Lee with a caring and alive church near her, with a specific pastoral contact. What an incredible call back!

Reyna—Texas, USA (Brokenness)

Reyna is broken hearted because her husband of 2 1/2 years

(although they've lived together since 2004), has left her for another woman. She is six months pregnant. Reyna went online on YouTube to find someone who could guide her to God and found our Prayer Line! In our follow-up call we gave Reyna the name and number of a Spanish Pastor and his wife in her city, suggesting Reyna contact them for encouragement and growth in the Lord. Also we gave Reyna Scriptures to look up online for her own spiritual nourishment and prayed with her. Through many tears Reyna expressed her gratitude for our call back and help!

Maxine—Nova Scotia (Grief/Loneliness)

Maxine was very broken in her first call to the Prayer Lines as her second husband had just passed away 3 1/2 days before. Her first husband passed away 20 years ago, and now her eldest son has Leukemia. Maxine has been finding life very difficult. We comforted and encouraged her with the truth of God's Word that because she has opened her life to Jesus Christ as her Savior and Lord, He declares, "Never will I leave you, never will I forsake you." (Hebrews 13:5) and "The Lord is close to the brokenhearted, and saves those who are crushed in spirit." (Psalm 34:18). She was so very grateful for the call back and knew she was going to make it!

Raymond—northern Manitoba (Broken Marriage)

Raymond said he is really hurting because his wife had left him. However, since he gave his life to the Lord he can see that his heart has changed. He and his wife have begun to talk, which is a good sign. They have seven children and I encouraged him to be the man that God can use, beginning in his own family. He was so grateful for the call back and said, "It's nice to hear from you, really makes me feel good." It's that personal touch that makes the ministry of Crossroads so powerful.

Roger—Ontario (Loss/Grief)

Roger began sharing that he found our Prayer Partner very helpful, that she identified with his loss and what he was going through because she also had lost her spouse to cancer! He is left with two children 13 & 10 years of age who are struggling with their grief too, and at times it's almost overwhelming. Roger is trying to be strong for them, but realizes he needs help!

He is dealing with regret over what could have been, as he and his wife had been unfaithful to each other. We shared with Roger the power and importance of forgiveness Jesus offers in order to release us from regret and condemnation. Recommended several helps in dealing with loss and a caring church in his area. It was an amazing call and Roger was so deeply grateful that 100 Huntley Street was there to help him in his darkest hour!

Juliana—British Columbia (Desperation)

Juliana is 19 years old and missing God in her life. She felt He was angry and mean because she had sinned too much for Him to take her back. Juliana has one 2 year old and is 7 months pregnant, both by the same abusive father. We spoke of the Father's unconditional love for her (John 3:16), unlike any human father's love, and that He is the God of "return" (Jeremiah 24:7). We encouraged Juliana to return to Jesus and connect back to church. We prayed with her and let her know it would be ongoing.

Carmen—Alberta (Abortion)

Carmen was raised with a religious background, but it didn't have any influence upon how she lived. Because of that Carmen has had two abortions and felt she was unforgivable. However, after being confronted with the reality of death she realized she needed help and called our Prayer Line to give her life to Jesus. At the end of our call back Carmen said, "I can't believe you guys are taking the time to take care of me. Thank you!"

Shahana—Ontario (Abuse)

Shahana has only been married two years but it has been very difficult as her husband has been both physically and verbally abusive. She finally had to call the police and he now has a restraining order against him. However, because they are Muslim she feels the pressure and desire for him to return. In her need she was watching 100 Huntley Street and wanted very much to know the love of Jesus in her life and opened her life to Him as the Prayer Partner made Him known to her heart. During the call back Shahana was asked if she would like a call from a Pastor at a caring church, to which she said yes! After the call the Pastor was contacted and he had a compassionate lady in his church contact Shahana. She has begun going to the church and really enjoys it, and is growing in her love for Jesus! She was so very grateful for the help she was receiving from 100 Huntley Street and the church we connected her to!

Camile—Jamaica (Deportation/Abandonment/Desperation)

Camile called from Kingston, Jamaica! While living in Canada she got involved with a man and became pregnant by him, (she already had a child by a different man). Through much deception by this man to the authorities she was deported. In great desperation Camile called our Prayer Line from Jamaica acknowledging she had made many poor choices and realized she needed to get her life right with God. We encouraged her to get back into the Word of God and prayer, putting Jesus first. In a subsequent follow-up call Camile shared that the Judge in Canada has ruled that she and her daughter are to be returned to Canada! This is a great victory and Camile is conscious it is only by God's mercy. She has determined to serve the Lord!

Georgina—Northern Saskatchewan (Family problems)

Georgina has great sadness and stress with 3 drinking sons in their 20's. She is a widow and her mother passed away recently. She is not a good reader and thus has trouble reading the Bible. We shared with her a couple of scripture verses and helped her spell out each word so she could write them down, then read it back. She was so very grateful. Georgina said, "If I didn't see your Prayer Line and call your number, I don't know how I'd have made it through."

Alice—Newfoundland (Sexual abuse)

A Priest in the Catholic Church sexually abused Alice when she was 5-6 years of age, then later by her own father! As a result she grew up with many doubts about God, who He is and what He is like, causing her to distance her from the church. However, she was watching 100 Huntley Street and in her pain called the Prayer Line. After compassionate ministry Alice opened her heart and life to Jesus. Follow-up has continued in helping her deal with damaged emotions through the mercy of Jesus our "wounded healer" (Isaiah 53:3).

Lynn—New York State (Loss due to suicide)

Lynn's husband was a State Trooper who had a nervous breakdown and later committed suicide. She said he was a tough cop who showed no affection. After he died she got involved with a man who showed her affection, but she knew it was wrong. Watching 100 Huntley Street one day she called the Prayer Line and found her way back to God. In one of our follow-up calls she said, "You're the best Prayer Ministry in all of North America! Thank you."

Reyhaneh—Ontario (Searching)

Reyhaneh is a Muslim who had a dream about Jesus, then became very happy when she discovered our channel and program 100 Huntley Street! We explained more of the gospel, why Jesus came and what He did on the cross.

Reyhaneh with open heart received Jesus! In a follow-up call we connected her to a caring, evangelical church where she has begun to go and be spiritually fed. In another follow-up call Reyhaneh said, "Thank you for your service and giving to people makes my life changed!" Her friends are now asking her, "Why are you so peaceful?" Her response, "It is because of Jesus!" Yes!

Irene—Nunavut (Illness)

Irene has had eczema for 18 years, and as a result, walked away from God. However, she realized life is too hard to handle without the Lord and called our Prayer Line to rededicate her life to Jesus. In our follow-up call she shared how that day she walked without pain! As I prayed she began to laugh with joy at the Lord's goodness to her!

Annie—Quebec (Loss)

Annie's fiancé died of a heart attack 8 years ago and she is still grieving his death. Gratefully a friend gave her our Prayer Line number and as a result of her call Annie gave her life to the Lord! We connected Annie to a caring, evangelical church near her. In a subsequent follow-up call Annie said, "everything has been so good since we talked last! I've begun reading the New Testament you sent me and feel so encouraged." Annie expressed such gratitude!

Vanessa—Ontario (Suicide)

A few years ago Vanessa's brother tragically took his own life. She was very close to her brother and it was profoundly devastating when she came home and found his lifeless body. Vanessa found it hard to recover, added to that her family and even her own son abandoned her. Life was hard and on top of all this emotional pain she lives with Multiple Sclerosis and its debilitating effect on her. Vanessa felt there was nothing to live for, however before harming herself she made that one call that would indeed be the most important...Crossroads Prayer Lines! Our compassionate Prayer Partner assured her of God's love for her and that life was still worth living. In a subsequent follow-up call we were able to reassure Vanessa that though others, even family may abandon us, there is one who "never will leave us, never forsake us." (Hebrews 13: 5-6) and that Jesus is that "friend who stays closer than a brother." (Proverbs 18:24). Vanessa has also been given information for Christian counseling.

Kendra—British Columbia (Suicide/Addiction)

Kendra had come to the end of herself. Heroin will do that. Sick of living, yet not really wanting to die, Kendra was tired of her addiction. Gratefully, rather than ending it all she called our prayer line! Our Prayer Partner helped Kendra find her way back to the Lord and experience his forgiveness. That same evening our first follow-up call was made to Kendra who now was going through "cold turkey" we assured her of our ongoing help and desire to connect her with a caring church that had a Celebrate Recovery program. She agreed to that and immediately we made contact with this church and the pastor in charge of Celebrate Recovery. He assured us that he would contact Kendra immediately and have one of their female leaders connect and stay in contact with Kendra. Our last contact with Kendra was after she was six days clean, as we trust the local church to practically demonstrate the compassion and healing of Jesus. This grants Crossroads a huge reach, literally "across the nation and around the world" to thousands of local churches who can be the hands and feet of Jesus to those who call and connect with us!

CHAPTER 8

A Strong Deterrent To Suicide

There is no question in my mind that in the home there is the potential to make or break a teenager.

Julie cried as she told me the story. She and other graduating senior girlfriends were at a slumber party celebrating that soon school would be over and they would be "free". Everybody chimed in to share their thoughts late that night as they relaxed in sleeping bags scattered across the room, but Brenda dominated the conversation. She kept talking about her problems. Not just one, two, or three. That night, all her problems spilled out. One after the other, Brenda expressed problem after problem. Finally, somebody told her to pipe down and let someone else talk. After everybody eventually dozed off, something motivated Brenda. Slipping out of her sleeping bag, she quietly made her way up the stairs to the bathroom while her friends comfortably slept. Once she had locked the door, she carefully wrapped the cord of a hair dryer around her neck and hung herself from the shower rod. Early the next day the door was torn down and Brenda was found. But, as with so many others, it was too late. In our minds, we see her struggling for life in the early hours of morning, we wonder why? Julie told me there were problems in Brenda's family. "If we had only known that night she was reaching out to us," she sobbingly commented.

Literally by the hundreds young people have approached me and told me they had either already tried suicide or were seriously considering it. Some youth show me their scars of past attempts or theorize methods of self-destruction. I have always responded with the exact same question to every depressed teen—why? Truthfully, I can say that at least two-thirds of all suicidal young people have responded to me with the word family in their answer as to why suicide was on their minds.

There is absolutely no question in my mind that in the home there is the potential to make or break a teenager. I tire of hearing speeches and reading articles about "delinquent" teenagers in North America. In reality, there are many troubled adults and extremely turbulent families in which teenagers' problems gestate to the point of suicidal expression.

The breakdown of the family, in my opinion, is the chief area of direct concern for finding answers to the teenage suicide epidemic. Yes, I know, some young people have mental illnesses. I am not discounting that fact. Did you know most suicides occur at home? Strange, isn't it? Many also begin at home, that is, the suicidal mind-set starts to develop in the home. In the environment that should breed security and comfort, many times things seem to go wrong for adolescents. Instead of peace, there is fear. Instead of harmony, there is discord. Instead of joy, unhappiness, replacing love is conflict. Often, suicidal ideation for a young person begins when a family lacks cohesiveness, cooperation, communication, and love. For those who succumb to depression, suicide becomes the final chapter in a sad, turbulent family story. I am not denying the fact that suicides have occurred in strong, stable homes, like the Stoufer's that you will read about in this book. But, more often than not, a child mirrors the complexion and quality of his/her family.

Scores of suicides and attempted suicides have no connection whatsoever to drug or alcohol abuse. Tragically, a significant number are linked to family problems. Insightful parents and intelligent teenagers should know about the potential or this kind of danger at home. And, again, even the best families are vulnerable in this area.

The great divide. No longer can we speak of the "typical family" in North America. In years past, that phrase described the traditional, middle class unit of an original father, mother, and children living together. Today, that combination represents a minority of North American homes. The combined realities of divorce, remarriage, single parent families, the new trend of millions of cohabiting couples, children born out of wedlock, has all created a far-from-ideal society. For many – perhaps most – teenagers, it is a very hard world in which to grow up and develop. Now social engineers, in the name of equality, want to redefine marriage, which will redefine families.

Same sex marriage has made significant gains throughout Canada and in an increasing number of states in the U.S. While President Obama described his opinion on gay marriage as "evolving," America's attitude on the controversial topic has been gradually shifting toward approval. The support is strongest among young people: Nearly two-thirds of adults born in 1981 or later favor same-sex marriage, according to a survey from the Pew Forum on Religion & Public Life. Demographers make it clear, it is only time until the vast majority of Americans will be in favor of same sex marriage. We have no data to review regarding how emotionally balanced or imbalanced children and teenagers will be in the homes of same sex parents, let alone polygamous or polyamorous families. Time magazine recently featured an article of how polygamous and polyamorous marriages and families, due to the gains of same sex marriage in various states and provinces, will seek the same equality and acceptance. One TV network reality show, now in multiple seasons, attempts to feature the normalcy of polygamous families. Within a decade it is foreseeable that the traditional boundaries of the family will be blurred. In this context, families will be comprised of two dads, two moms, a husband and two or three wives, and potentially two women and two men, etc. As most experts would agree, the implications of these new definitions of the family and how it relates to child rearing and emotional stability are simply untested. How all of this will play into adolescent suicidal ideation is fearful and unknown.

Divorce. In 1830, one in thirty-six marriages in the United States ended in divorce. In 1970, four out of every ten marriages ended in divorce. Today, as we know, one in nearly two marriages dissolves in the divorce court. It is astonishing to realize there are some geographic areas in the U.S. where the divorce rate now exceeds the marriage rate. Every 20 seconds a married couple file for divorce in the United States. A very troubling trend for the future is the reality that 60 percent of all divorces are filed by couples 25- to 39-years-of-age. It is also interesting to note that as the divorce rate increased dramatically from 1950 to 1980, at the same time the teenage suicide rate skyrocketed 278 percent. One relevant and reliable source indicates the number of divorces per 1,000 married women rose from 9.5 to 21.9 during the years 1954 to 1978, more than double.

In the last forty years our society has undergone more changes, at a faster rate, than any other period. Now, the digital age makes that entire metamorphosis look slow! This all presents added pressures on the family. Turbulent families, splitting apart, induces suicidal ideation. Teenagers sometimes blame themselves for their parents' problems. Too often, the physical, emotional, and spiritual support a child needs is woefully lacking by a divisive family or parents who have their own set of problems to deal with.

Did you know the statistics reveal there are 1.2 million

divorces in the U.S. every year? That means that every year, another 2.4 million people go through divorce! And if the average cost of divorce is $20,000 per couple that means that Americans are spending $42 billion (yes, billion) on divorce each year! The United States has the highest divorce rate in the world. Prior to the 1970s, divorcing spouses in many states had to allege that the other spouse was guilty of a crime or sin like abandonment or adultery; when spouses simply could not get along; spouses and their lawyers were usually able to negotiate "uncontested" divorces. The no-fault divorce revolution began in 1953 in Oklahoma; New York is currently the latest state to allow non-consensual no-fault divorce, in 2010. The median length for a marriage in the US today is 11 years with 90% of all divorces being settled out of court. Only eleven years of marriage does not even give children the time to grow up!

Canada is ranked eighth of thirty-four nations in the number of marriage that end in divorce. Statistics Canada no longer collects and crunches numbers on the country's annual marriage and divorce rates. The last year of data, in 2008, revealed there were 70,226 divorces in Canada, 43.1 percent of Canadian marriages are expected to end in divorce; 62.6 percent in the Yukon. Realizing there has been a rise in divorce of more than 100 percent, the proportion of teens that are impacted by the burden of a chaotic family has increased dramatically. It is not possible to overstate the trauma on teenagers when they watch two parents—whom the equally love—split apart and go their separate ways. When divorce occurs, teenagers are often hard-pressed to cope with the demands and transition. Their loyalties are strained because, in most cases, they do not want to fail either parent. Caught between a father and mother who have rejected one another, the child's sense of self-identity and worth is in question. ABC's *Nightline* reported the suicide attempt of a teen that had felt his divorced parents made him choose between them. He said, "I sort of feel sometimes that the fights that go on between my dad and mother pull me apart. So it's like I've got to choose sides. I can't—it's difficult for me to just stay in the middle and be pulled from side to side." Another teenager interviewed on the same program said of her parents, "they can't help me. They're children themselves."[26] With 1.2 million divorces in the U.S. per year, and over 70,000 divorces annually in Canada, millions of kids are thrown in flux. And with millions of young people each year experiencing the baggage of divorce and separation, we certainly see a contribution to youth suicide and attempts.

Remarriage. Trying to replace an original parent where there is a bond of love with a step mom or dad is, to some teenagers, impossible. Adapting to a new parental figure can get extremely complicated for a teen. In some cases, the stepfather or stepmother does not truly accept the teenager, who is a reflection of the original parent no longer in the home. Getting up and going to bed every day in this awkward, unacceptable environment may invite suicidal thoughts.

"Our home is all screwed up now. It will never be the same again. I would rather go back to the fights my original parents used to have than this."

"Why not kill myself?" another teen wrote. Some remarriages have worked beautifully, due to the maturity of the parents, their gracious understanding, and patience. Regretfully, a significant number of other remarriages have failed. Couples in second marriages have a significantly higher rate of dissolution (through divorce or separation) than first marriages. Researchers tell us that 75 percent of divorced persons remarry within a few years. People who have divorced and remarried multiple times tend to be relatively impulsive and nonconformist. Furthermore, people who are already familiar with divorce tend to be more accepting of it than people who have stayed married. In second marriages, partners also often have to deal with additional complications that do not exist in first marriages, like combining families.

Remarriages involving stepchildren have a greater rate of dissolution than those without. Add to this group of divorce/remarried people other remarriages that result from the death of spouses, it is calculated that about eight million children/young people in the U.S. now live in stepfamilies.

Some couples try having a child together to unite their families more strongly. But having "yours, mine, and ours" doesn't always work, and for many, divorce is inevitable. Picture the teenager, trying to develop socially, going through puberty, caught in this web.

Single parent families. According to the U.S. census bureau, 12.6 million children under the age of eighteen live with only one parent; that figure represents 20.1 percent of all children. It is easy to see why natural problems are evidenced in the single parent home. Because of the parent's need to put bread and butter on the table, the teenager does not have the natural accessibility to the single parent that is working. The pressure of needed finances is present. Also, the absence of the other parent, whether it is father or mother, leaves the teenager deprived of a balanced development. In some cases, the single parent has multiple short-lived romances with the opposite sex. The teenager viewing this activity becomes confused, and personal insecurity is a byproduct. Romantic interests of a parent become a major threat and can be viewed by the teenager as real competition. Later this can become an ongoing problem if a remarriage results.

Undeclared divorce homes. In millions of two-parent households, there is undeclared divorce, and the children inevitably sense the division. Mom and dad are together legally and practically, but not emotionally. Countless teenagers have told me through tears about the friction between their parents. And for some they are sure of the cause: themselves! Steven Stack is an Adjunct Professor of Psychiatry, and Full Professor of Criminal Justice, Wayne State University, Detroit, MI. He is also Director of the Center for Suicide Research, a registered non-profit corporation in Troy, Michigan. Dr. Stack points out that research on the families of teen suicide victims indicates they are more likely than other families to be characterized by recurrent yelling, less affection, a pattern of hostility, nagging parents, a symbiotic relationship between parent and child that permits no autonomy, intolerance of crisis, depressed and/or dominant mothers, neglect of children for a career, too much or too little discipline, and geographic mobility that breaks up social networks.

> "The chaotic family increases psychological states amenable to suicidal behavior: depression, guilt, anxiety, hopelessness, low self-esteem, and so on. For example, years of hostility between parents can leave the child emotionally deadened, lagging behind his peers in psychological development." [27]

I have always said the greatest gift a father can give his children is to love their mother. The greatest gift a mother can give her children is to love their father. I have been in love with my wife, Cristie, since the day I saw her in October of 1978 in Holland, Michigan. Subliminally, my three children have developed great strength and confidence by how much Cristie and I love each other. Parent, what kind of love for your mate have you been emulating to your children?

There is no question that problems in the home are carried by a teenager internally and leaves them plagued with questions about the vitality of life. One woman in Ohio handed me a poem she wrote about a neighbor family whose son completed suicide. She told me she watched the family deteriorate through several years until the son died by suicide. When he was young the family was much closer, but eventually things changed. Her poem highlighted three areas of the young man's life: elementary school, middle school, and college. It read:

Once on yellow paper with green lines

He wrote a poem ...

And he called it "Skip"

Because that was the name of his dog and that's what it
was all about.

And his teacher gave him an "A" and a gold star

And his mother pinned it to the kitchen wall

And showed it to his Aunt.

And that was the year that his sister was born

And his parents kissed all the time ...

And the little girl around the corner

Sent him a postcard with a row of X's

And his father tucked him into bed every night

And was always there.

Then on white paper with blue lines he wrote

Another poem ...

And he called it "Autumn" because that was the season it
was and that's more

more what it was all about.

And his teacher gave him an "A" and told him to write
more clearly.

And his mother told him not to hang it on the kitchen
wall

Because it had just been painted.

And that was the year his sister got glasses and

His parents never kissed anymore

And the little girl around the corner

Laughed when he fell down with his bike

And his father got mad when he cried to be tucked in.

On a piece of paper torn from his notebook

He tried another poem

And he called it "?" because that was his big concern

And his professor gave him an "A" and a

hard searching look, and his mother didn't say

anything at all because he never showed it to her.

And that was the year he caught his little sister necking

on the back porch and the little girl around the

corner wore too much make-up so he laughed when

he kissed her—but he kissed her anyway.

And he tucked himself into bed at three in the morning

with his father snoring soundly in the next room.

And that's why, on the back of a matchbook cover he tried

tried another poem ... and he called it

"Absolutely nothing" because that's what it was all about.

And he gave himself an "A" and a slash on each wrist

and hung it on the bathroom door

because he couldn't make it to the kitchen.

A big deterrent to youth suicide is a dad and mom that have a happy relationship. You can't trick teenagers or pull the wool over their eyes. If their parent's marriage is raunchy and the home wall-to-wall hell, they will know it. It will mar their development and, for some, breed suicidal thoughts. I am positive that a loving, balanced home in most cases will be just the influence necessary to avert suicidal disaster. It is up to the parents to instill security or insecurity in a teenager.

Communication breakdown. Seventeen-year-old Julie felt cut off from her parents. Her final, distressing words give just a glimpse of the despair that covered her like a shroud.

> Dear Diary,
>
> No one knows I'm alive or seems to care if I die. I'm a terrible, worthless person and it would have been easier if I'd never been born. Tabby was my only friend in the world and now she's dead. There is no reason for me to live anymore.

Eileen's poor communication with her parents almost resulted in her premature grave. She lives in Alabama now. She wrote to me:

> Recovering from a suicide attempt is a long process. If my parents had only listened to me when I first talked about it, I might have been helped before I tried to kill myself. My folks knew that I was thinking of suicide . . . I had expressed my desire [to die] several times before taking an overdose. . . I suppose they might have thought it was just a stage I was going through . . . But, it wasn't a stage. I was acting out of total despair. My parents just couldn't believe that their daughter tried to take her life. I came within minutes of death. The fifty pills I had taken had been in my system for an hour and a half before I was discovered and rushed to the hospital. So, Jerry, tell parents to love their children as if it was the last day they could spend with them. Tell parents to listen to their teenagers. It could save them a lot of heartaches later on in life & the lives of their kids.

What causes a communication problem? At the heart of it, I believe it is a breakdown in trust. Whenever trust is lessened or lost in a relationship, communication suffers severely. Teenagers and their parents can relate in a wholesome, positive way only if they trust one another. And this means there has to be room for failure and forgiveness. Let me illustrate.

A teenage girl who had sex on several occasions with her boyfriend, broke up with him, and confessed what was going on with her parents. Her father spouted, "All you are is a little slut anyway. That is all you are ever going to be. If you had been a decent girl, you never would have done it in the first place. Why do you tell us now? Because you think you're pregnant, isn't that it?"

That wasn't it, after all. The girl was reaching out to be consoled and understood in the aftermath of a poor decision and upsetting experience. Instead of consolation, she received condemnation. She ended up being destroyed, ground in the gears of her father's anger.

What really hurts is the realization that so many lives are lost because of poor or nonexistent communication between teenagers and parents. It doesn't have to be this way. Bridges, strong and enduring, can be built across the so-called generation gap. But it takes work, commitment, flexibility, and acceptance – on both sides.

Missy, a high school student from Texas, wrote me a six-page letter. Here is an excerpt:

> If we would've talked [when I spoke at her school] I would have told you that I have one of the best homes and one of the worst. My parents give me almost anything I want but they don't trust me. Sure, I've made mistakes that weren't too intelligent, but mothers says we should forgive people who make mistakes. Why should I be around if they can't trust me? What can I do if I'm not responsible enough to make my own decisions? You know, I tried to kill myself for the first time in the 7th grade. Fourteen years old and I tried to kill myself. . .

Missy wrote of four attempts to take her life. She is a top student in her school and a high achiever.

The tyranny of expectations. At a high school commencement in Waverly, Massachusetts, a grade twelve graduate received his diploma, stepped to the microphone, and said, "This is the American way." [28] Then taking a revolver from under his gown, he raised it to his head and pulled the trigger. He survived, fortunately, but a dramatic statement was made.

What drives a young man or woman to such extreme action? In some cases, it is the culmination of mounting pressures—internal and external—that have been building for years. Finally, in volcanic fashion, they erupt in a display of raw emotion, and sometimes, bizarre behavior.

One of the most intense pressures bearing down on many young people is the parental expectation level. Even without knowing it, many parents attempt to press their children into their mold, using a variety of techniques. From some affluent, highly successful parents comes the pressure for their son or daughter to succeed—to make it to the very top. This could be in academics, athletics, or even dating. The mounting pressure becomes a steamroller to many young people, and suicide is there way of escape. The traditional past habits of many parents are forced on some young people. "You have to go to Yale, Princeton, or the University—your father did." "If you are not first-string on the football squad, you will be less than what your dad was."

In the high school years, the pressure to succeed materially comes from some affluent parents. Teenagers are told that there are only so many quality jobs out there and they had better get going now if they are going to be successful. The pressure is on to be perfect. Yet, I know young people who could care less about owning a BMW, Mercedes, or wearing Prada. They are saying, "I don't share your value system—

back off." Parents need to give their children breathing room and let them develop their own skills and talents.

Seventeen magazine cited the story of Jamie whose parents had outsized expectations. Early in life, he learned he could please them only by what he achieved. When he did well at school, they loaded him with compliments and praise. They became cold and distant when he did not do well.

After high school, Jamie went away to one of the Ivy League colleges. He did badly and tried to explain about wanting to change schools, but his parents would not hear of it. He could not meet the academic load and felt he could not live up to their expectations. Jamie killed himself at college and left a note for his parents that said simply:

I knew I would fail you

One pressure tactic used by parents is promoting comparison. "Why can't you be like your sister? Your brother doesn't act like that." What's wrong with you?" Statements like these should be banned from a family's vocabulary. They are damaging, and they can be deadly.

Another negative behavior I see is the compulsion of some parents to live out their dreams through their children. The achievements they could not attain become the brass rings toward which they relentlessly push their kids. For teenagers with any measure of individuality, this is often insulting. For those who are highly sensitive, it is threatening. More than one embattled teenager has told me, "I don't want to be like them. I can't meet their expectations." A sixteen-year-old said, "My parents know two words: *faster* and *hurry.*"

Is anybody home? In the years following the Second World War, an increasingly larger percentage of mothers have taken jobs outside the home. Many mothers, particularly those who are single parents, have no alternative. Economic realities demand they earn a living to meet their children's needs. For many, however, this pattern was established when the teenager was a baby. Many mothers pride themselves on how quickly they could be back to work after their newborn's birth. Subsequently, the little one was farmed out to babysitters and day-care facilities. As a result, that teenager may not have bonded with his mother when he was an infant —this is deprivation some psychologists believe is critical in the further development of suicidal teens. There is an entire, ever growing study in the "biology" of suicide that is most fascinating.

CHAPTER 9

Sex and Suicide

One seventeen-year-old Atlanta girl complained, "If you say
no, you're a tease, and if you say yes, you're a slut."

M ary, a grade ten student, said, "I wasn't able to
handle the pressure. I was part of a group in
middle school that was into partying, hanging out, and
drinking. I started to have sex with my boyfriend and it was
a real downer. It was totally against what I was, but it was
important to be a part of a group. Everybody was having sex."

Is Mary's dilemma typical? We live in a sex-saturated
culture. No one loses out more than our young people.
Exposure to sexual content in movies lead teenagers to
have sex earlier and to participate in riskier behaviors. That
is not the conclusion of some preacher behind a pulpit. A
study published in Psychological Science, a journal of the
Association for *Psychological Science* reports:

- Among movies released from 1950 to 2006, roughly 85
  percent contained sexual content.

- Seventy percent of the sexual acts depicted in movies
  released from 1983 to 2003 occurred between newly
  acquainted partners, 98 percent included no reference
  to contraception and 89 percent resulted in no

consequences.

- Sexual explicitness of PG-13 rated and R-rated movies have increased over the past decade.

- Adolescents sometimes seek out sexual media, with 57 percent of U.S. adolescents ages 14 to 16 reporting that they use media as a primary source of sexual information.[29]

What are we doing to our youth? Only nine percent of sexual content in movies contained messages promoting sexual health. The evidence suggests that adolescents' sexual attitudes and behavior are influenced more by movies than by other forms of media, the study clearly reported.

Newsweek had a cover story that encapsulated how promiscuous teenagers are with their peers:

> In the absence of moral guideposts, teenagers have developed their own rules of the love game. They no longer frown on their peers if they are sexually active. Once chastity was something to be guarded or lied about when lost. Now an uncommonly virtuous teenager lies to protect the dirty little secret that she is still a virgin. There is more pressure than ever for a girl to 'get it over with,' as one teenager put it."[30]

I have seen firsthand this situation and have heard the same kind of sordid report from kids in hundreds of schools internationally. It is lamentably true.

The Centers for Disease Control report in 2005, 47 percent of high school students (46 percent of female high school students and 48 percent of male high school students) reported ever having had sexual intercourse. In 2005, among those high school students who reported being currently sexually active, 23 percent (19 percent of females and 28 percent of males) reported having used alcohol or drugs the last time they had sexual intercourse.[31]

High school students today are obsessed with going all the way sexually. For the majority, sexual expression is a part of sincere but short-lived relationships. It is very common for teenagers to have multiple sexual encounters with various partners long before graduation from high school. Enter the college university scene and sexual hook-ups are rampant. And, sexual liberation has rapidly increased since the late sixties and early seventies. Sharon, a grade twelve student said:

I'd say half the girls in my graduating class are virgins. But you won't believe those grade nine and ten students. By the time they graduate, there aren't going to be any virgins left.

One seventeen-year-old Atlanta girl complained, "If you say no, you're a tease, and if you say yes, you're a slut." A Johns Hopkins University study revealed that nearly half of the United States' 15-to 19-year-old girls have had premarital sex and the numbers keep rising. Think of that for a moment. One of every two high school students is sexually active, and in some geographic areas of America the percentages are even higher. The National Center for Health Statistics reports that only one American woman in five waits until marriage to begin sexual activity.

On the other hand, I've been appalled at the callous attitude of many teenage guys. Some boast about how many girls they've "laid" or "popped." This kind of if-you-love-me-let-me egomania is deplorable because it damages deeply and can even lead to death. When I speak in high schools, I often say, "Remember girls, no guy will ever love anyone he does not respect." To most girls, sex is an expression of commitment, and when they are dumped for some other erotic playmate, the rejection is overwhelming.

Sexual activity among teenagers, of course, leads inevitably to pregnancy, which in turns leads to an upwardly spiraling abortion rate. Currently, 45 percent—almost half—of teenage girls who become pregnant have had an abortion. This startling figure accounts for nearly a third of the abortions performed in the United States. "Abortions seem to be most common among the affluent. Upper-middle-class girls look at abortion as a means of birth control," says Myra Bennett, a county health official in southern Illinois. [32] And some girls become so despondent, wanting neither to be pregnant nor to have an abortion, they opt for suicide. Thus, two lives are taken.

Christine Langlois reports in *Canadian Living* what is true of young people whether you live north or south of the border:

> More than 80 per cent of North Americans have their first sexual intercourse as teenagers. It's a major step into adulthood and one that a teen should feel comfortable discussing with his parents. But few do feel comfortable. Many kids even say they're reluctant because their parents are too serious about sex or take too long to answer their questions. They also complain that parents don't talk about the associated feelings. [33]

The social consequences frequently include rejection by insincere boyfriends and lovers and scorn from friends or relatives. After one of my high school assembly presentations, on girl said to me, "My dad repeatedly calls me a whore, and my relationship with my mom is just not the same anymore."

And again, that report, like many others, reminds us that parents are the most powerful influence on sex and relationships with their children—if, if, they get involved! Cristie and I raised two girls, Danielle and Jenilee. I must admit there were a couple of relationships with boyfriends in high school that I simply stopped. I remember Jenilee, crying, so mad at me. Later she came to me and said, "Dad, thank you for making that decision when I couldn't." Both of our girls were virgins when they married. That did not happen by accident. It took a lot of love, parenting, and survelliance! In every part of the country, I have discovered that parents have an aversion to talking with their teenagers about sex. Some never bring up the subject, and others wait until it's too late. (I see a strong parallel with the refusal of parents to discuss suicide with a son or daughter who is exhibiting warning signs.) I don't blink in telling parents that if they think they can avoid discussing sex and everything will be okay, they are dead wrong! Blanketing themselves with the reassuring thought that it won't happen to their Susie is sheer foolishness.

Sadly, some parents actually expect their teens to be victimized, and they feel powerless to do anything about it. One mother said, "Down deep I know it is going to happen sometime no matter what I say. Is my oldest daughter still a virgin? I don't really know and the tough part is I don't really want to know." I can say firsthand, teenagers themselves tell me for the most part; their knowledge of sex was obtained neither at home nor in school. Many tell me they learned about sex from friends or from and older brother or sister. And, a lot of teenagers learn all about sex from experimentation.

An interesting footnote to the sexual revolution among American youths is that many teens are not as knowledgeable as they think they are. Significant percentages are misinformed or unaware of the scientific facts of reproduction and even the use of contraceptives. But they are thrust into the fast lane, and because of peer pressure, they must strive to keep pace with their sophisticated friends. On the other hand, there are teenage girls who get pregnant intentionally, for a variety of reasons – some are getting even with their parents, and others simply want someone to love. Whatever the intent, the outcome is seldom what the teenager imagined it to be.

Moreover, the sexual revolution seems to have moved from the college campus to the high school and now to middle school. Never will I forget a tiny girl who came up to me after my talk to a thousand teens in an eastern city. "Everybody wants me to do it," she said. Leaning down, I asked her to repeat herself. "Everybody wants me to do it," she said again. "Do what?" I asked. "Have sex," she said with a wide-eyed expression, as if to ask, "Is it okay?" Physically, she was far from maturity. I wondered how she would ever make it through high school without suffering irreparable emotional harm.

Dr. Nancy Clatworthy, who was a professor at Ohio State University, studied teenage sexuality for more than a decade. She sees in the United States:

> "A slide in moral values. There isn't any big deal to being a virgin today. It isn't one of those high value items. It is simply a question of teenagers not seeing anything wrong with it. They see it on television, in books, the sexuality obvious that it is just assumed as a form of self expression." [34]

At Dunedin High School in Clearwater, Florida, a girl with a spiked haircut approached me. "They call me a dyke here," she said. "Really?" I replied. "Are you gay?" She smiled and said, "Sure, I like it better with girls." I have heard similar statements from other girls in other schools across North America, most of who looked straight but were far from it. It is alarming to realize researchers believe one in ten teenagers is gay—a statistic of propaganda.

I have witnessed a growing popularity of homosexual and bisexual lifestyles among teenagers. When I spoke in Lima, Ohio, one grade eleven student became so disturbed he jumped up and ran out the door. Later, he told me he was gay. His story substantiates the claim of researchers that gay teenagers are among the loneliest kids in the country.

Many teenagers caught in homosexual activity have poured out their hearts to me. Usually, their homosexual affairs began with a guy masturbating another guy or a girl caressing another's breasts. More experimentation leads to sexual activity, and when then happens, the guilt is often cruelly unrelenting. Many suicide notes document this fact. I must also add, most young people I have encountered who chose a homosexual lifestyle experienced sexual abuse, and most never told anyone about it.

When I had just completed an interview on KMBZ radio, one of the DJ's asked me, "Have you heard of autoerotic asphyxiation?" I responded, "Yes, and it is growing across the nation with teenagers." It has been called the American teenager's best kept secret. In New Orleans, youths nicknamed the practice *fantasy*. In Texas, one teenager described it to me with the word *ecstasy*. This bizarre fad is practiced not only when a teenager is alone and thrill seeking, but also when psyching out at parties. Tragically, dead bodies are left hanging after having experienced an unexpected death by suffocation.

What is autoerotic asphyxiation? A report in the Journal of the American Academy of Child Psychiatry defines autoerotic asphyxia as "self hanging while masturbating to achieve sexual gratification." Of course, a teenager engaging in this practice is not intending to kill himself. Instead a crazy pleasure is the object. In autoerotic asphyxia, the supply of oxygen to the brain is restricted, usually by a noose around the neck, as a way to heighten the pleasure of masturbation. The constriction of the neck results in heightened sensations described as "giddiness, light-headedness, and exhilaration." While practitioners of sexual asphyxia may take elaborate precautions in the belief that they will not endanger themselves, as long as they prevent actual choking or suffocation, in a moment of excitement they can unintentionally apply too much pressure to their necks, resulting in unconsciousness, complete hanging, asphyxia, and death. All research says that victims are heterosexual males, most under twenty-years-of-age. They usually fit under the classification of the t-personality—the thrill seekers.

Police in New York investigated apparent cluster suicides. One death in particular intrigued them, and they questioned whether it was, in fact, a suicide. The parents found their teenage son hanging naked, in the bathroom. They also discovered semen on the floor. The police report concluded that the victim died accidentally in sexual experimentation.

In Ohio, there is a mother of another teenager who died in the same manner. She commented that it was time to bring this horrendous conspiracy of silence to an end. Adolescents and others, the mother begged, should be warned of the dangers of this practice. Parents should know how to detect warning signs before move young lives are needlessly lost, she cried.

Forensic pathologists have known about autoerotic asphyxia for years, but it has never been a public issue. Until now. When a death occurs from autoeroticism, it shocks families. Doctors, and sometimes-even police, tend to hide the truth to protect the family from embarrassment by labeling it suicide.

I grew up watching the TV show, Kung Fu. It was all about the discipline of the mind coupled with Chinese martial arts. David Carradine, the 72-year-old actor was found dead in a Thai hotel room closet in an intricate web of ropes—one around his neck, another around his genitals and the two tied together, according to Thai authorities. "Sex experts say that Carradine's advanced age suggests that he may have been a lifelong practitioner of the secretive and dangerous practice, one that can go fatally awry. Los Angeles Superior Court documents of Carradine's divorce put online by The Smoking Gun show that his most recent ex-wife, Marina Anderson, accused the actor of 'deviant sexual behavior which was potentially deadly.' The alleged behavior wasn't described in the court documents." [35]

Rarely, does auto-erotic asphyxia get listed as 'cause of death' when the coroner files the report of a sexually bizarre fatality.

Estimates are that 500 to 1,000 deaths of this nature occur every year in the United States. Reports say that most autoerotic asphyxia deaths are misdiagnosed as suicide or homicide or else covered up by the family because, again, of the social stigma that surrounds a sexually motivated, sometimes accidental, death. There is currently no way to get an accurate count of the number of autoerotic fatalities. The codes by which coroners classify these deaths contain no such category for autoerotic asphyxia deaths.

Massachusetts studied all adolescent suicides in a four-year period and found that hanging was the second most frequent method of death. It makes us wonder how many were true suicides and how many were accidental. One authority alleged that some of those deaths were, in reality, accidental autoerotic deaths. One FBI report, a study of 132 autoerotic deaths by asphyxiation, found that many of the victims had periodically used the technique to heighten orgasm in masturbation. They had always been able rescue themselves before death occurred—until the last time. One doctor said, "You may do it right forty times but on the forty-first, you make a wrong move and die."

When they are found, victims may be naked or may be wearing underwear or female clothing. Often, pornographic literature is nearby as well as various rescue devices, such as a knife to cut the cord or a key to unlock the chain. A towel or cloth is placed around the neck to prevent burns and marks. Extremities are girded with ropes or chains. When discovered, victims are suspended by the neck, caught by unexpected death.

There is a sensitive area of the carotid artery in the neck that feeds the brain. By turning the wrong way, a person can become unconscious and death is inevitable. One expert pointed out that the risks of sexual asphyxia are not well known and it could be viewed as no more pathological than driving a car at a high speed.

"My pleasure is closely connected with fear," said one young man who was interviewed anonymously on TV by having his features blacked out and his voice distorted. "I'm afraid of choking. In a state of fear, life, and lust are compressed into a narrow space. The more pressure exerted by fear, the more vivid the pleasure gets inside." Some researchers think that nearly all those who repeatedly engage in this behavior suffer from a psychological disorder known as sexual masochism. Autoerotic asphyxia fulfills masochistic need for punishment that arises from the guilt associated with masturbation. Obviously, this is a twisted, decadent practice. I hesitate to mention it because of the suggestibility of some youth reading this book. But, parents and kids must be warned. This is a deadly practice.

One estimate is that more than seventy-five percent of teenage guys masturbate. How many of these young men will be drawn to this deadly practice? I mention this not to sensationalize, but again to provide caution. Parents should watch for bloodshot eyes, marks on the neck, disoriented behavior (after the young man has been alone for a while), and possession of or fascination with ropes and chains. Sounds bizarre, doesn't it? And, yet, quite tragically, it is happening. The mother of one victim said she had never heard about it. Until her son's death she had never heard of autoerotic asphyxia. These parents called the school principal, urging him to warn other students, but nothing was done. The next year another boy in the same school died by autoerotic asphyxiation.

One fourteen-year-old Houston guy did not know about autoerotic practices either, at least not until he managed to get his hands on a copy of Hustler magazine. There, step-by-step, he learned the technique of autoeroticism. He tried, and it cost him his life. The family sued Hustler, and a federal grand jury ruled the magazine was responsible for inciting the young man's death.

||||||||||||||||||||||||||||||||||||

CHAPTER 10

Liquid Enemy

*Alcohol abuse is killing 2.5 million people each year
and governments must do more to prevent it,
according to the World Health Organization.*

A large group of teens gathered around me after I spoke to the student body of Wolfson High School. One by one, they shared their frustrations and asked penetrating questions. The last one I talked to was Christy, an attractive dark-haired grade eleven student. By outward appearances I would not have singled her out as a troubled person. She sobbed, "Jerry, I feel so guilty. My best friend Laura is dead." I asked for details and Christy related the horrible story that devastates her.

Christy and Laura were stopped at an intersection, waiting for the traffic signal to change. A flashy sports car eased up next to them, and Laura caught a glimpse of the handsome guy behind the wheel. Whispering to Christy to take a look, Laura lowered her window and struck up a conversation. Before long, the man invited them to meet him later that evening on Jacksonville Beach.

They met and had some drinks together. After a while they left the bar and strolled down the beach joking, laughing, still drinking. About 9:30pm, they were about to head home when the fellow asked Christy to ride with him. Christy, thinking that Laura was too intoxicated to drive, suggested, "Laura, you ride with him, and I'll follow you." But the young man was drunk, too. He sped recklessly out of the parking lot.

As the late-model Ferrari he was driving climbed the J.B. Bridge, Christy said they must have been going at least eighty miles per hour. At the crest of the bridge, the car swerved into the path of oncoming traffic. There was a spectacular, head-on collision. Christy, who had been trying to keep up, arrived at the scene of the accident within seconds. She jumped from her car and raced to the viciously smashed Ferrari, screaming, "Laura, get out, Laura, get out!" But then there was an explosion, and the car burst into flames. Her friend Laura was burned beyond recognition, her body reduced to a charred mass just three and a half feet in length.

Christy, still weeping, concluded, "The kids here at school straightened up for about a week, and then everybody was back to drinking and partying." She shook her head in bewilderment. I nodded knowingly, because I've heard the same comment many times.

Alcohol abuse is killing 2.5 million people each year and governments must do more to prevent it, according to the World Health Organization.[36] It is almost incomprehensible how many people die due to the liquid, legal drug of alcohol. The grief of a family member who is an alcoholic cannot be overstated. My mother suffered from alcoholism. A very patient, loving husband stuck with her until she was set free. For many families no deliverance from this bondage comes.

Adults drank too much and got behind the wheel about 112 million times in 2010—that is almost 300,000 incidents of drinking and driving each day.[37] Motor vehicle crashes are the leading cause of death for U.S. teens, accounting for more than one in three deaths in this age group. In 2009, eight teens, ages 16 to 19, died every day from motor vehicle injuries. In 2009, about 3,000 teens in the United States aged 15–19 were killed and more than 350,000 were treated in emergency departments for injuries suffered in motor-vehicle crashes.[38] Alcoholism statistics on drunk drivers show that drinking and driving results in one injury every minute and one death every 32 minutes. Drunk drivers are costing the United States approximately 50 billion dollars every year. Alcohol costs so many so much; their health, family, friends and their community.[39]

Again, drinking while driving is the number one teenage killer with thousands of deaths annually. The National Highway Traffic Safety Administration estimates that half of all traffic deaths involve drivers who have been drinking. This points to an even greater problem—the menacing evil of teenage alcoholism.

I struggle to comprehend why few who campaign so vigorously against drunk driving dare to speak out against teenagers using alcohol. In fact, I have gotten the implication from some that "it's all right to drink, just be sure you don't drive." That's crazy, to put it bluntly! Unbelievable numbers of kids are fueling a riotous lifestyle with alcohol.

After speaking in Ft. Lauderdale, Florida, one night, I was approached by a paramedic who seriously said, "Jerry, don't ever stop what you are doing. Keep warning the kids. I shot these pictures just a few days ago. I want you to have them." I guessed the man thought I had been around enough to see about as much as there is to see. When I flipped through those color photographs, I almost got nauseated. They mirror a guy and a gal who were going together. The couple went out that fatal night to have fun with a bottle of alcohol and Quaaludes. The mixture was too much. As they were racing down the highway, they must have been laughing, music playing, and living it up. The pictures reflected agony and pain. The vehicle sailed over the side of the Interstate and slammed into the riverbank below. The posture of those two young people, in that automobile-turned-coffin, is a sight that will remain in my mind as long as I live.

The girl's head was down by the accelerator petal in the driver's seat. Her body was upside down and wrapped around the steering wheel. Her drenched dress had slid down her body and was barely clinging to her at navel level. Her leg had shot through the windshield and lifelessly dangled outside the car. But it was her head and arm that created such emotion within me. It was outstretched toward the door as if she was pleading and screaming for someone to pull her out as the river filled the car to her eventual death. Her boyfriend's body was catapulted to the backseat. His head was cocked in an unnatural manner. Because of Drugs and alcohol two more young lives were snuffed out prematurely.

The most widespread drug problem in North America is not the abuse of LSD, amphetamines, cocaine, crack, or marijuana. Alcohol, the socially acceptable and readily available legal drug, is our worst offender.

A star basketball player at Sprayberry High School in Marietta, Georgia, raced up to me after I finished speaking to the school's 2,200 students. Without saying a word, he grabbed me by the arm and led me behind a partition in the gym. Then when we were alone, he looked at me, with tears streaking his cheeks. "Jerry," he said gravely, "I'm an alcoholic. I just wanted you to know I'm an alcoholic. I know what you're talking about."

I have had kids tell me they started drinking before school, and begin their first hour drunk. Many are simply reflecting their parent's lifestyle. If a father or mother drinks abusively, why shouldn't a son or daughter? Some teenagers have admitted to me that their first drink came at the bar conveniently located in the family den or from the kitchen. Others tell how they were introduced to alcohol by a jovial relative at a family get together. Without discipline and restraint at home many teens are predisposed to abuse alcohol themselves. Parents addicted to alcohol have no hope of helping their alcoholic children until they first get themselves straightened out.

As I left Bonnabel High School in New Orleans, I noticed an unusual display on the school lawn. It was a demolished automobile, every foot of it crumbled and crashed. The windshield was shattered with only a few shards remaining. The interior was a nightmare of ruin. A sign in front of the wreck read DON'T DRINK AND DRIVE. Transfixed by the sight, I found myself imagining the screams of those who died in the impact.

I thank God for the thousands of high schools across North America that have chapters of Students Against Drunk Driving. I wish every school had a chapter. However, we must face the brutal fact that drunk driving is not a cause but a symptom. Drinking is the root problem, and until our society has enough fortitude to denounce it, we are going to continue to see thousands die needlessly every year.

A teenage alcoholic, like any alcoholic, commits slow suicide. The body is damaged, and years of life are reduced. Practically speaking, drinking is a suicidal act. And should the alcoholic be killed in an accident while under the influence, that, too, is suicide. If someone else's life is lost, that's murder.

Why They Die: Curing The Death Wish in Our Kids

CHAPTER 11

Drugs and Death

The abuse of drugs and alcohol induces deaths by suicide.

A s I walked down the steps of West High School in Anchorage, Alaska, some students shout at me, "Hey, Jerry! Come here. This is our Across the Street." They were referring to a story I told in the assembly two hours earlier. I had mentioned I used to get high right across the street from the school at the place my friends, at the time called, "Across the Street." Although it was September, it was already quite cold in Anchorage. I looked at those kids, shivering in the woods, cupping joints, and doing drugs and thought what a waste.

On Friday night of that week in Alaska, we held a rally that was open to the community. Twenty-two hundred people filled that auditorium to stand-room-only capacity. The atmosphere was electric with anticipation and concern. After the meeting concluded, I was exhausted so I sat down on a folding chair at the end of the platform. Many distraught people came to talk; some were very distraught. One of the most pitiful encounters was with a young man named Joey. High on acid, his eyes frighteningly reddened, he had to contort his mouth to get the words out, "I can't get it together, man,' he said haltingly. I knew he was wasted, and it made me so sad. All I could do was tell his friend to make sure he got home safely.

Canadian youth are turning on drugs at a rate that exceeds their American peers. Partnership for Drug Free Canada reports:

- Twenty six percent of Canadian youth have smoked marijuana (that is one in four).[40]

- Some of the highest percentage comes from kids in higher income families.

- Twenty percent of teens have taken a prescription drug to get high. Seventy five percent said they stole the drug from home.[41]

- Almost twice as many young people admit to driving after taking drugs over alcohol.[42]

- The mean age of Canadian youth first engaging in illicit drugs is 12.6 years old.[43]

- Canada has a significantly higher incidence of usage of illicit drugs among grade ten and twelve students than the United States of America.[44]

The abuse of drugs and alcohol induced deaths by suicide. About 50 percent of all suicide attempts involve alcohol and illegal drugs (including those who use alcohol or drugs in their attempt or test positively for alcohol or drugs at the time of the attempt). About 25 percent of completed suicides occur among drug abusers and those with alcohol abuse problems. The suicide rate of people under age 30 is increasing, largely because of substance abuse among young adults. In the U.S. more than 50 percent of teens that commit suicide have a history of alcohol and drug use. Many teens that are considering suicide suffer from depression. Studies have shown that young adults who drink heavily have an increased risk of suicide in middle adulthood. People who are dependent on alcohol or drugs have an increased risk of death from accidents, disease, and suicide. In fact, suicide is among the most significant causes of death in both male and female substance abusers.

Again in Canada, suicide is the second highest cause of death for youth aged 10-24. Each year, on average, 294 youths die from suicide. Many more attempt suicide. Aboriginal teens and gay and lesbian teens may be at particularly high risk, depending on the community they live in and their own self esteem. The cause can seldom be attributed to one single factor, such as the death by suicide of a rock star or family break-up. It may be a routine event or an overwhelming one that overloads a vulnerable youth's coping mechanisms. As well, new research suggests that there may be a genetic link to suicide. A family history of suicidal behavior should be taken into account, if for no other reason than the young person may have been affected by this behavior in the past. And, a family history of mental illness, drug or alcohol abuse can cause a young person to be predisposed to suicidal ideation. The abuse of drugs and alcohol, in a sense, is a cloaked suicide killer.

Look no further than the singing sensation Whitney Houston. Most people would have the opinion that Whitney did not die by suicide. This is another example of how death certificates by the thousands never hint at suicide by people who die due to the excessive abuse of drugs or alcohol. Technically, that is correct. However, as we have learned, when a person becomes hopeless they succumb to addictions, depression, and live, what out what I call a suicidal-behavior. Autopsy results revealed Whitney's death was caused by drowning because of effects from heart disease and cocaine abuse. She was found by her assistant face down in the bathtub at the Beverly Hilton Hotel in Los Angeles, and had been dead about an hour. She suffered from atherosclerotic heart disease and emphysema, and had a "perforation in her posterior nasal septum," which is a common symptom of chronic cocaine use. All of her natural upper teeth had been replaced with dental implants. There was cocaine, marijuana, Xanax, and Flexeril (cyclobenzaprine/muscle relaxant) in Whitney's body at the time of her death.

Michael Jackson died due to "acute Propofol intoxication," and his death was ruled a homicide, not suicide, after a toxicology report discovered that the powerful sedative Propofol (Diprivan) and other sedatives ultimately caused Jackson to go into cardiac arrest. He weighed only 136 pounds (62 kg) with a height of 5'9" (175 cm). The report showed there had been a desperate struggle to save Jackson. He had chest bruising and cracked ribs from CPR and a mechanical device known as a balloon pump had been inserted into his heart to try to restart it. There were four injection sites found above or near his heart, where rescue workers repeatedly shot adrenaline into his heart in an attempt to restart it.

Jackson died at his rented Los Angeles mansion on June 25, 2009, after his personal physician, Dr. Conrad Murray, administered the anesthetic propofol and two other sedatives to get the chronic insomniac to sleep, according to court documents. Propofol, normally a surgical anesthetic used in operating rooms, acts as a respiratory depressant and requires constant monitoring. Arnold Klein told CNN that Jackson used an anesthesiologist to administer propofol to help him sleep while he was on tour in Germany. CNN said the anesthesiologist would "take him down" at night and "bring him back up" in the morning during the HIStory tour of 1996 to 1997.[45] Jackson had several tattoos, all of them cosmetic, including dark tattoos in the areas of both eyebrows and under his eyes, and a pink tattoo around his lips. Here, again, is another tragic example of the destructive impact of long-term drug abuse. It is common knowledge that Michael suffered from the estranged relationship with his father, Joe, who he had virtually cut-off.

One of the most talented singer-songwriters Britain has produced, 27-year-old, Amy Winehouse, was found dead in bed in her London flat. She drank herself to death. That was the ruling of a coroner's inquest into the death of the Grammy-winning soul singer, who died with empty vodka bottles in her room and lethal amounts of alcohol in her blood – more than five times the British drunk driving limit. Coroner Suzanne Greenaway gave a verdict of "death by misadventure," saying the singer suffered accidental alcohol poisoning when she resumed drinking after weeks of abstinence. "The unintended consequence of such potentially fatal levels (of alcohol) was her sudden and unexpected death," Greenaway said.[46] Recalling Winehouse's addiction, music producer, Paul O' Duffy, commented, "She didn't have an off switch. You or I have a few drinks and then we're done. She wasn't."[47] Like Kurt Cobain, Amy, was impacted by the divorce of her parents.

I have met young people all over North America who, knowingly or unknowingly, are flirting with death by listening to their friends, instead of the facts, of how abusing drugs and alcohol can kill.

Joey was really no different from a thousand other kids I have dealt with in every state and province in North America. I have now spoken in over 900 cities throughout North America and Europe. Young people come to our events high, sometimes hallucinating, incessantly snuffing—driving the coke deeper in their bodies. Some are curiously blatant. At one high school in Columbus, Ohio, a student smoked a joint right while I was speaking. Perhaps he was being defiant, perhaps he was crying out for help in a marked way.

Nicholas came up to me on the playing field of the Jack Russell Stadium in Clearwater, Florida. Breaking down crying, he said, "I'm sick, Jerry, I'm sick. Please help me!"

In an Iowa farming community I met Bobby, a short stocky grade ten student. Bobby was a speed freak. While we talked, he could barely sit still. He told me that one day at school during his lunch break a pusher lured him to a cellar stairway and turned him on. By the time I met him, Bobby was hooked.

Brad, a handsome young man in a southern high school, told me that his addiction was PCP (known as angel dust or killer weed) and it caused him to act in a bizarre, frenzied manner. His parents were so alarmed that they placed him in a psychiatric ward of a local hospital. While he was hospitalized, some of his "friends" smuggled PCP to him. When a nurse found him, Brad was trying to flush his head down the toilet. He was not far from death, yet he still had to be physically restrained.

One expert told me his research indicates that an average American child who turns on to drugs begins the escapade at age eleven! While I was speaking in San Francisco, a nervous faculty member approached me and asked, "Mr. Johnston, are you going to speak to the elementary students in our area?" I replied, "We did not plan on it. We tried that in Georgia and felt it went right over their heads." She countered, "You need to change your mind. We have experienced pot smokers here in grades five and six. They need your message!

Years ago, First Lady Nancy Reagan, in her foreword to *Marijuana Alert*, wrote:

> When I visited a third grade class in Atlanta, I asked how how many students had ever been offered marijuana. I was shocked when almost every little hand—of boys dressed in Cub Scout uniforms and girls in jumpers— went up. As I traveled throughout the country, this scene has repeated itself over and over again."[48]

The Weekly Reader conducted a survey of 500,000 young students that produced some alarming results. It was reported by 39 percent of fourth graders that "using drugs is a big problem among kids our age." And 30 percent said that "the main reason kids start to use marijuana is to fit in."[49]Unlike other national surveys, the *Weekly Reader* poll focuses exclusively on grades four through twelve.

Our public schools in the United States and Canada are infested with drugs. This is more a reflection of our culture than the public school system. Drugs are everywhere. In every prison where I have spoken, i.e., Leavenworth Federal Penitentiary (infamously nicknamed "The Hot House"), the Kentucky State Prison (one of America's bloodiest prisons containing numerous inmate misfits), among others, inmates have told me drugs are readily available.

Columbia University reports, "Significantly, three-quarters of the 12-17-year-olds surveyed said coming across photos of other kids drinking or smoking on Facebook and other social networking sites encourages them to want to get high—and almost half the teens say they see photos of kids passed out or using drugs. Compared to kids who haven't seen pictures like these, kids who have are four times likelier to have smoked cannabis, more than three times likelier to have drunk booze, and almost three times as likely to be cigarette smokers."[50] The 17th annual back-to-school teen drug-use survey from the National Center on Addiction and Substances Abuse at Columbia University (CASAColumbia) is shocking and documents American high school students say that around 17 percent of their peers use drugs, alcohol or cigarettes during the school day—a total of around 2.8 million teens.

In major metropolitan areas, drugs are as big a problem, sometimes bigger, than alcohol. In rural America, the number one craze is still drinking to get drunk. Breaking it down further, I have discovered in the middle- to upper-middle-class communities cocaine is the substance of choice. In the low-income inner-city area, teenagers will use anything they can get their hands on. Young people have told me how they sniff gas, glue, inhale aerosol spray, and even take a chance with crack. Anything to get a buzz. Of course, there are those poverty-stricken areas that use expensive drugs, but their means of getting them is almost always stealing.

- When I speak to high-school students, I purposefully use colloquial terms from my days of getting high. I use words like . . .

- *stoned* (high on drugs)

- joints (marijuana cigarettes)

- *hitting* (inhaling on a joint)

- *rush* (the euphoric feeling drugs bring)

- *buzz* (the initial high experienced from a drug)

- *munchies* (strong appetite from taking drugs)

- *coming down* (the depression after a drug-induced high)

- *burnout* (the physical need for a more powerful drug)

- *dime bag* (sandwich-size plastic bag with a "two-finger" measurement of marijuana)

- *lid* (a "three-finger" measurement of marijuana)

The kids know what I am talking about. Often I can tell that some teachers are listening intently to figure out what I am saying while the students are elbowing one another as if to indicate, "this guy knows what he's talking about. He must have been there."

Drugs, unfortunately, are here to stay, I'm afraid, and teenagers are going to be tempted by them. When they give in and experience the highs and lows produce, one authority wrote:

By the time he's 15, your child may know more about the contemporary drug world than you ever will. Teenagers crave experience, and once they're deeply involved with drugs, drug 'educators' won't offer them anything that comes close to the actual taking of them—the instant, chemical-induced feeling that problems have vanished. [51]

The pressure for a kid not using to turn on is often unrelenting. The inexperienced teen will likely have at least one friend who urges involvement. Drugs are in virtually every school in North America, and at one point or another your son or daughter will be asked, "Do you want to get high?" If it's not the friend your son or daughter hangs out with, then it might later be their boyfriend or girlfriend: and for the sake of the relationship, they might say yes to drugs.

Mom or dads, grandparents, intervene if you see your children or grandchildren abusing drugs or using alcohol. Give them the facts—the straight facts—that drugs, including the liquid can kill, and they can facilitate a slow descent to die by suicide.

CHAPTER 12

A Plea To Parents

*I kept asking God why He would allow something like this
to happen. I searched my heart, asking,
What did I do wrong? How did I fail Aaron?*

For nearly 35 years, I have been married to my wife, Cristie. In my estimation, she is the most perfect person in the world. I have told her many times, "You are filled with such goodness." How the Lord blessed me with her I will never know. Cristie virtually raised our children as I traveled the world speaking to over three million students in over 900 cities. God used all those school assemblies, speaking events, and the literature we distributed, to save thousands of young people from suicide. I have received hundreds of letters from students all over North America that reference how crucial our efforts were in their rescue from suicidal impulses. Christie and I have three very talented, gifted children, and now four beautiful grandchildren. As we raised three children, in retrospect, I see how crucial the role we played as parents was and still is in their lives. I can distinctly remember in Jeremy, Danielle, and Jenilee's lives critical moments where they truly needed us to overcome some challenge or the negative influence of one of their peers. Scores of other parents have shared with me how they lost their son or daughter to suicide.

In every case, my heart has been filled with such compassion for them. Nothing could be more painful for a parent. Let me encourage you how to continue living after the suicide of your son or daughter.

A friend of mine was cutting paper on a large trimmer when his hand slipped into the blade's path. In an instant, the edge of his index finger was severed. Though in moderate shock, he managed to wrap a handkerchief around the wound and hold it there tightly all the way to the hospital. Since the index finger is amazingly sensitive, he was in agony. After treatment in the emergency room, he was released. Recuperation was not easy. For several days he had to keep his injured hand elevated at all times to restrict the flow of blood and lessen the pain. He had to take strong medication. And still the finger throbbed incessantly, sometimes feeling as if it were a thermometer about to explode. In subsequent weeks he made eight visits to a plastic surgeon for reconstructive treatment.

Today, my friend's finger looks perfectly normal. It is not deformed in any manner. But he tells me that because of nerve damage, it always has a tingling sensation. The initial pain is gone, but there is a constant reminder of that one traumatic moment when part of him was cut off.

Though it may at first seem strange, I see in my friend's experience a remarkable parallel to the process a family goes through when one of its members commits suicide. Initially, there is indescribably anguish, deep beyond imagination. Then there is a slow, arduous healing period. Various "medicines" must be taken to endure the trauma, and in my opinion prayer can really sustain you in these days of healing. The help of other family members and friends is essential as reconstruction continues, if ever so tediously. Finally, everything appears to be back to normal, at least to outsiders. But it isn't. It never is, nor can it be. When there is emotional nerve damage, the tingling reminder of past hurt is always there.

Do you remember how I shared with you in the first chapter the problems I endured as a youth and came close to the brush of death? That part of my life seems so incongruent to my career, which has been filled with so many blessings, and my academic career that resulted in obtaining an earned doctoral degree from Acadia University's Divinity College in Nova Scotia, Canada. Instead of trying to hide my past or being embarrassed about it, I chose to share it with others in hopes of helping them. I can't even begin to tell you how gratifying it is to know there is not one but scores of other suicidal young people and parents who are alive today because God gave me the courage to be open. This is the exact way I recommend for parents, grandparents, brothers, and sisters to heal after the suicide of their family member. Don't hide and act like it did not happen. Don't blame yourself —each person, ultimately, has volitional will to make decisions. Instead, use the death of your son or daughter, or loved one to minister to others. Do you realize how many people you could help? A lot of people will not listen to a psychiatrist or preacher, but they will listen to you because you have "been there." Reach out to other parents and their children. Be willing to share your experience with the schools, churches, and organizations in your community. Don't become bitter, become better. "It is what it is," but God can use it to minister to others. You are going to discover a strange reality, that by helping others through their difficult experiences, you will find comfort yourself!

In the hundreds of opportunities I have had to counsel suicidal teenagers, I tell them: "Think about the damage you are going to cause. You will leave behind loved ones riddled with guilt, overcome with despairing thoughts, puzzled over questions never to be answered." I put it bluntly: "The ones you leave behind will never, never be the same again." And I add: "They will blame themselves for your self-centered act of final defiance. What's more, if you kill yourself, you may cause a brother or sister or friend to take the same foolish step."

When I spoke to the student body of Liberty Junior High School in Liberty, Missouri, there was understandably rapt attention. Four teenagers in that typically Mid-western city had committed suicide within months of each other. The entire community was asking, "Why is this happening to us, to our children?" During my talk, I was unaware that in the audience sat the grieving mother of a fifteen-year-old boy who had taken his own life. He was the second in that fateful string of four senseless deaths. After my address that afternoon, I met Barbara Stoufer and learned about the devastating loss of her son, Aaron. Later, in the living room of the Stoufer's home, I heard the whole story. So relevant and compelling, I asked permission to share it. Mr. and Mrs. Stoufer graciously agreed to my request.

Bear in mind that Aaron Stoufer lived in a balanced, happy home. He did not use drugs or alcohol. Never did he suggest to anyone that he might take his own life. Yet Aaron's death was part of that cluster of four teen suicides in Liberty.

Dennis Stoufer, Aaron's father, recalls:

> The morning of April 3 was the last time I saw Aaron alive. Minutes before he board the bus about 7:00a.m., he and I joked and teased each other. He poked me in the side with his elbow and smirked, "Fat man, leave me alone." It was his way of kidding me for being a little overweight. I yelled, 'Have a good day,' as Aaron left for school. Moments later I headed East on a marketing trip for my company.

> I stopped by at Terre Haute, Indiana, about four hundred miles away. While unpacking my business supplies in the hotel room, the phone rang. Dr. Rogers, my neighbor, was on the other end, 'Dennis,' he said sternly, 'there's been a shooting.' I was still taking in the words when he added, 'Barbara, Mary, and Travis are

fine. But Aaron's dead.' My mind went blank, and my emotions froze as I heard myself mumble, 'Oh, no.' My body became instantly numb. Somehow I managed to ask, 'Where's Barbara?' She came on the line. 'Dennis, come home. I need you,' she said in a hollow, desperate voice. After that, Dr. Rogers said something else, but I don't remember what. But I did grasp the fact that Aaron had shot himself.

Across Interstate 70 on the way home, I cried almost continually. I kept asking God why He would allow something like this to happen. I searched my heart, asking, What did I do wrong? How did I fail Aaron?

Arriving about 2:00 in the morning, I let myself into the house and went into Aaron's bedroom where he had killed himself. I fell down on my knees at the edge of the bed and wept bitterly. I prayed for courage, for peace, for help. Both my mind and body were in shock.

Barb was at a neighbor's house down the street. I went down to see how she was taking everything. Our two other children, seven-year-old Mary and four-year-old Travis, had been taken to stay with other friends nearby. I phoned to see how they were. Then determining it would be better for Barb to stay where she was, I returned to the house. Another friend came with me, and stayed for the next few hours.

I couldn't sleep. In my anxiety I went fifty-four hours with rest. Finally, in my zombielike, exhaustion overtook me.

Confusion swirled in my mind. I recall thinking, *Two plus two just don't add up to four anymore.* I could not make normal decisions. Even deciding what to eat for breakfast seemed an impossibility.

Gradually, I began to move out of the shock. But I could

not understand why Aaron did not reach out to us. Then I started to blame myself again. At the same time I tried to compose myself so that I could think about all sorts of practical questions: What was going to happen to Mary and Travis? What about funeral arrangements? Who should tell Aaron's close friends? I really did not want to cope with any of those things, but I knew it had to be done.

Hundreds of times since then I have asked, What if? What if I had tried to talk to him more? What if I had not driven away that morning? A year after Aaron's death I saw the movie *Back to the Future* and broke into tears because, unlike the people in the film, I could not go back and relive things and change the outcome.

Even Travis and Mary have asked, 'Didn't Aaron like us enough?' 'Was he mad at us?' 'Did Aaron hate us?' 'Did he kill himself because of us?'

'No, of course, not,' we would say, then remind them of the many times when Aaron would take them out to play in the backyard or the neighborhood. Aaron did not talk to his best friends about taking his life, and apparently he did not even hint at the possibility. I find myself going back to his childhood, wondering what I did wrong or where I failed. Even now, I am still reliving the past. I've retrieved from memory all the times I grounded him or spanked him for things I didn't approve of. I've asked, Did I somehow provoke it—the thought of killing himself?

"I remember one incident when Aaron was four. He darted across the street, and I had to run after him. It frightened me so much; I whipped his bottom fifteen or twenty times. He went inside, sobbing his little eyes out. I have wondered if that was physical abuse or if I punished him too hard. The memory troubles me. Yet, about one year before his death, I overheard Aaron recount the whole episode to a friend. He said, 'Yeah, my dad whipped my butt to show me he didn't want me to get injured out in the street.' I realized, with great pain, that I would never know what was really in his mind and how that experience really affected him.

"As a surviving father, I am deeply concerned about teenagers who are at crisis points and thinking about suicide. I urge them; I beg them, to give their parents a chance. So often, a teenager will think that mom and/ or dad don't understand. I remember feeling that very way when I was growing up. But mom and dad often do understand. Try; just try to talk to them. Suicide is a one-time, one-sided statement but the trauma inflicted upon those left behind is felt time and time again.

"I think about Aaron every day. On some occasions, like his birthday, the thoughts of him are so overpowering. I even find myself counting days since his death. For the rest of my life, I never want a day to go by that Aaron isn't a part of it. I want the memory of him to create in me an ever-deepening awareness of life's preciousness. I want it to make me kinder, more loving, more sensitive to my other children. I want his death to have an enduring significance."

The words of Dennis Stoufer grip my heart as if it were placed in a vise. Each thought he shared turns that vise a notch tighter. Pressed and pressured, I am moved to examine painstakingly my relationship with my own children. As a father, I can identify with Dennis, and I can learn from his excruciating experience. I know that is what he desires.

Aaron Stoufer also left behind a heartbroken mother, Barbara. Listen now to her words:

"It started out like a typical school morning. Everyone was rushing around, getting ready, eating breakfast.

Aaron finally made it out the door and headed for the bus stop. He came home happy that afternoon about 3:15p.m., joking around the way he often did. A few minutes later he overheard a conversation about my getting a baby-sitter for the next night. That upset him. He reminded me that he was fifteen and a responsible person.

" 'You don't trust me anymore,' he said. 'Is that it?'

" 'Aaron,' I replied, 'we can talk about that later.' I was in a hurry because I had some errands to run, and I wanted to get back before dark. My answer wasn't unusual because at night we regularly had discussions.

"Many times we would sit and talk after I put the two younger ones to bed. Our real feelings would then come out. Aaron would tell me things he wouldn't share with his father. He talked about his girlfriends, about the things they would say, and I think he felt hesitant to relate that to Dennis. Especially when his father was on the road, Aaron and I would talk in the evenings. So, he understood when I said we'd talk about it later. But I didn't get that time with him, and he never gave me a chance to explain.

"I did not realize how upset Aaron was. I thought it was just a disagreement, or a little disappointment, like the difference of opinion when I'd want him to wear a different shirt to school. That day, though, he became quieter and wasn't joking as much as he normally did. Looking back, I believe his feelings about the situation worsened. When we came back from errands about 5:00p.m., Aaron went to his room.

"A short time later, I was startled by banging and pounding noises from Aaron's room. In a violent emotional outburst he was destroying everything he could get his hands on, smashing objects against the wall, tearing shelves down, acting wildly. He had never done anything like that before.

" 'Stop it, Aaron!' I yelled. I raced into his room and yelled again. He kept throwing things. I grabbed his shoulder and shook him. 'Did you hear me?' He nodded and looked away.

" 'Clean this up. I'm very upset that you've broken some very valuable things.' I walked out of the room and headed for the bathroom where the other children were getting cleaned up. It was nearly six o'clock. Behind me, Aaron evidently left his room and went over into our bedroom.

"In our bedroom we kept a .22 Magnum. It was a weapon Aaron had fired numerous times. He was an excellent marksman and knew the damage a bullet could do. Aaron went straight to that gun. I heard a terrible sound, like the popping of a loud balloon.

"When I heard the shot, I turned and raced back into the bedroom. The strangest feeling came over me. I had heard people talk about the angel of death, and that day I sensed his presence. Something was definitely there. As soon as I saw Aaron's body, I turned around. Because of the noise, the other children had followed me.

" 'What happened,' Mama?

' 'Just—just go back to the bathroom. I'll be there in a minute.'

" 'What was that awful noise?' Mary asked.

" 'Just go back. I'll be right there.' I felt a terrible surge of panic within me, a dreadful numbness. Without any conscious thought I ran across the street to the Rogers' house. Dr. Rogers is a medical doctor, so I desperately needed his help. I knocked so hard the door flew open by itself. Dr. Rogers was at home. I blurted out what had happened, and he raced ahead of me across the street.

" 'Call 911—the emergency number!' he shouted. I phoned, and the paramedic unit arrived within minutes. By then, Travis and Mary were crying, not understanding what was going on but sensing that things weren't right. I wanted to calm them down and comfort them, but I couldn't even do anything for myself at the time.

"I went into shock, overcome with disbelief. Everything seemed so unreal. I started calling my church. 'I need you now,' I kept saying over and over to them. 'Pray, please pray like you've never prayed before.' I groaned out repeatedly, 'God, help us, help us get through this.'

"The full brunt of tragedy hit me when the doctor came out of the bedroom. He looked directly at me and said, 'Aaron is dead.' Dr. Rogers is a good friend, and he'd always been straightforward with us. A wave of weakness engulfed me, and I started to fall. Dr. Rogers grabbed me. Irrationally, I struck out at him. 'No! No!' I cried.

"Later I went to a neighbor's house and did get a little sleep. I woke up about 5:00a.m. in the morning and went back up to the house and into the bedroom. I knelt down and prayed, pleading with God to help us through this. After a long time in the bedroom, I did feel more peaceful. That was the beginning of God's peace filling the void in my heart left by Aaron's death.

"We have what I always considered a basically good family life, and never did I imagine anything like this happening to us. And for it to come so suddenly, without any warning.

"Some dear friends took care of Travis and Mary and gave them a lot of attention, helping in those crucial days. About two months later, Mary started to have seizures. The doctor thought it was due to stress. She's still on daily medication. Shortly after Aaron's death, Dennis's mother died. Then my grandfather died. To Mary, it seemed that everybody was dying around her. We learned much later on that she had overheard a police officer saying that there had possibly been a murder. She tortured herself, wondering if someone had been in the house or if I had shot her brother.

It was several weeks before Mary started talking about Aaron's death. That's when I learned that she and Travis had gone in and seen their brother's body when I ran across the street. It was very difficult for her, but she managed to relate everything that had happened that night. There was an obvious relief, but she cried long and hard. Still, the hurt was there, and for weeks afterward Mary would start crying for no apparent reason. Occasionally, she even had nightmares.

"Another boy in Liberty had taken his life, and I had talked with Aaron about it. I now think Aaron may have toyed with the idea of suicide after that incident. I had talked with him the night of the other boy's death.

" 'Did you know the boy?'

' 'Yes.'

" 'How well?'

" 'Kinda good, but not like a friend.' Then he said it was a bad thing, and he didn't want to talk about it anymore.

"The day of Aaron's death, he had seemingly had a good day, according to his teachers, his girlfriend, and his schoolmates. And, ordinarily, when he got into an argument with me, he'd go outside and work it off or kick a soccer ball around the yard. He'd vent his frustration on something else. There was just nothing for us to suspect his getting made enough to do something so severe. We never saw him so charged up emotionally as he was that night.

"The hurt never goes away. You start learning to live with it and accept that it's going to be there the rest of your life. But still it hurts. Ours is definitely a labored existence, though I'm better now than a year ago. "

"After Aaron died, I considered suicide myself. *Why not?* I thought, in my depression and confusion. Quite often I slept a lot or at least tried to. That was a hardship on two little ones because they were not used to my new behavior. I had always gotten up and fixed them their breakfast. I had always washed their clothes, and the house was kept clean. All of that changed for a while. It was hard to do housework, hard to work, hard to do anything."

"Somehow I made it, finally deciding I couldn't hurt any worse. I had such a void in my life because Aaron and I were close. Or so I thought. But were we, really? Thoughts like these tormented me for a long time. Some friends would tell me, 'It's time to get on with your life.' But the words didn't help. In fact, they made me feel worse. Finally, though, after about a year and a half, I began to feel more energetic. "

"I struggled with a few thoughts about the stigma of Aaron's death on us. But I didn't feel that I had to explain anything to anybody about what had happened. Some things still bother me. Like noises. Certain pops or shattering sounds cause the memories to roll back over me. It reminds me of that gun going off. Being a mother and losing one of your children causes such emptiness. I learned the value of talking about it, and those who were willing to simply listen helped me.

"Almost every day I see Aaron's friends when they get

off the bus. Sometimes they look toward the house. For them it's not the same, because Aaron's not here anymore. They still ask questions when I talk to them. 'Do you know why he did it?' or 'Could we have done something to prevent it?' Some have even said that they've come by the house in the evening and glanced up, wanting to see his image in the window of his room.

"Every day I still wonder, what if I had done something in a different way, would it have made a difference? If I had stopped and talked instead of saying we would talk later. If I had been more sensitive to his mood, or loved him more, would he have been kept from taking his own life? I don't know how to answer my own questions, yet I must live with them every day.

"Aaron brought much love and joy into our lives. I'm glad he was here for fifteen years. I want his love to live on and help me be a better mother and wife and friend. Maybe if I can use what I've learned over these difficult times, I can be a better person. The "ifs" are endless, as is the hurt in not seeing his smiling face and enjoying his presence."

Dennis and Barbara Stoufer have joined me on more than one occasion and shared their poignant thoughts with audiences. Their words and feelings have helped so many thousands of people, and they have received therapy by their selfless, honest thoughts from the suicide of their son. Again, let me encourage parents who are reading this book to reach out, as difficult as it might be, and share your story with all of its unanswered questions with other people. Many communities across North America now have Survivors of Suicide support groups. Find one and join it. The American Foundation for Suicide Prevention (www.afsp.org) has numerous resource materials to help a family, individual, or school cope with the suicide of someone they love.

I am constantly asked by parents, "How can I better relate to my teenager?" Other moms and dads have asked me, "How can I be a better parent?" Frequently, they ask, "Help me navigate my child through our world with all of its many challenges." In my own parenting, and now grand parenting, I have endeavored to apply 10 key principles and I wholeheartedly recommend them for you:

1. Don't be naïve. Always be aware and stay aware of what is going on in your child's life. Know their friends by their first names.

2. Be informed. There is simply too much information available on suicide, drug and alcohol abuse, sex, communication, etc., for any parent to say, "I didn't know what to do!" Read, talk to other effective parents, and stay teachable in your parenting.

3. Start Listening. The greatest parent is the greatest listener. Let your children talk whenever about whatever, whenever they want to. Become creative about communication with your children. Take them alone on a trip, to a sporting event, or a quiet lake or mountaintop and let them talk. If they are not talking to you, I can guarantee you; they are talking to somebody else.

4. Be discerning. You don't have to be a rocket scientist to figure out if your son or daughter is abusing drugs, alcohol, sexually active, depressed, or losing interest in life. Don't be afraid to lovingly ask questions. Care enough, at the right times, to confront.

5. Embrace them. What we have learned from pediatric wards of hospitals must be practiced the rest of your child's entire life—hug them, hold them, kiss them, and let them feel the embrace of your love.

6. Model the Message. I have rarely met a negative

kid, who did not have a negative parent. Vice versa, visionary, happy parents often have visionary, happy children. If you have a drug, alcohol, mental health, or spiritual problem—get help because it can and will affect your children.

7. Care Enough to Correct. There is a difference between correction and punishment. Every child needs the security of a parent who cares enough to do something about their disobedience.

8. Nurture their dreams. Dreams and goals are what get us out of bed every day and look through our challenges and adversities with hope. Teenagers complete suicide when they have lost the dream for their life.

9. Help your child discover their T-alent, A-bility, G-ifts. God created every child with unique, special skills and gifts. When I was 17, I told my Mom I was going to have a preaching "LP record" someday (remember those days). She said, "I know you will." And, the next year my sermon was captured on vinyl, preached in one of the largest churches in America in my peach suit! My parents have been saying to me every day since, "Jerry, we know *you will!*" My parents gave me my self-confidence! Give this priceless gift to your kids.

10. Pray with them. Spiritual values and a personal relationship with Jesus Christ is a powerful antidote to poor decisions and temptations that can ensnare your kids. Nothing gets us closer to a person than regularly praying with them!

CHAPTER 13

"See You In Hell"

*"Tina, it's not your fault. Mom and dad, it's not your fault.
I'm not free. I feel ill. I'm sad. I'm lonely."*

Drugs, alcohol, sex, too early, and at the wrong time... it can all lead to death. As I have personally witnessed, this is serious stuff. Every time I see a dead teenager's body, sit with grieving parents and tell them their son or daughter has taken their life, or observe a young person, still alive, yet mentally and physically impaired the rest of their life by a failed suicide attempt, my heart yearns to do more to prevent this tragedy. And that is why I cannot stay away from using this gift God has given me to reach kids. Every death by suicide is preventable. This is why I dedicated the rest of my life to rescuing youth and helping parents and families find the abundant life Christ has promised. I will still speak in schools, conduct events in churches and communities, and give kids hope! I will warn them about the dangers that can pull them down. I identify with the words David Livingstone, the great missionary to Africa, penned, *"Some wish to live within the sound of a chapel bell; I want to run a rescue mission within a yard of hell."* Too many of God's people don't care about the hurting—I do.

Stepping briskly to the stage, I turned to face the thirteen hundreds students of Hanaford High School. Just as I had done hundreds of times before in schools across North America, I began my address:

"Jay was sixteen-years-old when his parents found him, face down, on the floor of his bedroom. Next to his body were a gun and a suicide note. It read like this:

> Dear World,
>
> I don't want to get my hair cut. I don't want to tend kids or see Tina at school on Monday. I don't want to do my Biology assignment or English or history or anything. I don't want to be sad or lonely or depressed anymore. I don't want to talk, sleep, move, feel, live or breathe anymore. Tina, it's not your fault. Mom and dad, it's not your fault. I'm not free. I feel ill. I'm sad, I'm lonely. One Last request. . . all my worldly possessions go to Debbie as a wedding present.

After reciting those dreadful, haunting words, I was puzzled by the student's reaction. Usually, such a crowd would become respectfully silent and remain attentive throughout my lecture. Not the teenagers at Hanaford High School. Gawking at me in apparent disgust, they were openly disturbed by the words I had quoted. Many of the girls began to cry aloud, some sobbing uncontrollably. I knew I had hit a nerve, but I didn't know what it was. Several faculty members showed uneasiness and uncertainty in their facial expressions. Somehow I had said something desperately wrong.

As I concluded, the audience gave obligatory but empty applause. After the principal made a few brief remarks, the student body was dismissed to the next hour's classes, and I was left wondering about the negative response I had received, unlike any school before. Over the dull roar of students filing out, I heard someone call out my name. An obviously distressed teenager stared me coldly in the eye and demanded,

"How could you have given Jay's suicide note here?"

Intrigued, I replied, "I quote that note every time I speak to students."

"Didn't you know Jay went to this school?" For a moment he hesitated, studying my face. He continued, "Jay Adams— he was my best friend, and this is one of the other notes they found next to his body." Nervous with excitement, he pulled a paper from his wallet. It had been folded nearly to the size of a matchbook. As he carefully opened the note, I could see the distinctively sloppy handwriting of a teenage boy. The note said:

Dear Steve,

I am sorry for what I have done but Robert and Mom made me think. Will your mom still have wanted us to be friends? I don't know. Tell Missy I love her and I hope she can pass science. Make sure you never be as dumb as I've been. Make friends and don't let them play that tape before my funeral.

Friends,

Jay

Instantly, assessing the message, I realized what had happened. Steve and his fellow students at Hanaford High School thought I had quoted the suicide note of Jay Adams one of their classmates who had recently taken his life. I quickly interrupted, "Wait a minute, Steve. The Jay I quoted was not your friend. He lived in another city. He was a different Jay."

Steve's face tightened, slightly from embarrassment I'm sure. Then he blurted out, "I don't know why he did it. He didn't give me the slightest warning that he was going to kill himself. He was my best friend!" Steve turned and walked away, lonely and dejected, still grieving.

Steve reminded me of countless other teenagers I had met in other schools, kids struggling to understand the senseless death of a friend. I remembered well the hurt that ached throughout my being when some of my high-school friends died needlessly. That day in Hanaford High School, watching that young man shuffle mournfully away, I had no solace in the fact that our stories had been confused, only a double sadness in realizing that two young men with the same name were gone forever. But that was not the last I would hear of Jay Adams.

Within a five-day period I spoke twenty-one times to public school assemblies, civic groups and community gatherings in one county. My Life Expose address was causing no small stir, as revealed by the stinging reality of suicide and the craziness of getting stoned and smashed. Administrators, civic leaders, parents, and students alike were responding positively to the message.

In just a few years, I had been on over twenty-two hundred campuses in more than 900 cities. I had spoken to at least three million American high school and college students. My odyssey had taken me to every state and every social level. I've listened to the frightful stories of young people struggling to survive in crime-infested ghettos. I've seen the tear-streaked faces of teenagers who live in big houses. I've heard countless stories of wasted lives, horrid accounts of drug addiction, bizarre behavior, and suicide. Whenever possible I always talk one-on-one to the teens in my audiences. It teaches me what is really going on in this country, and it keeps me from becoming just another professional speaker. Chronicled in my mind are innumerable incidents, but none is more riveting than the story of Jay Adams.

On Thursday night of that hectic week in Hanaford, the phone rings in my associate's room. Answering it, he hears a woman's quivering voice ask, "Is Jerry Johnston there? I need to talk to him really bad. Tell them this is Jay Adams' mother." I'm unavailable, but arrangements are made to meet her the following day.

After speaking to a crowd of twenty-two hundred at the Fairgrounds Arena, we are detained by people wanting to talk. Finally managing to get away, my associate and I headed for the hotel. As we greet Mrs. Adams in the lobby, it's obvious she has had a drink or two to kill the time. She is noticeably nervous, and her palm is damp with perspiration as we shake hands. We sit down in a quiet corner nearby. Without hesitation or restraint, the story of her fourteen-year-old son comes rushing forth like floodwaters through a burst dam.

It becomes clear almost immediately that Jay is not the typical teen suicide. Straight-A honor student, athletic, admired by others. Not exactly a person predisposed to take his own life. Or was he? Already I'm beginning to ask, Why?

Mrs. Adams hands me the framed portrait of a handsome young man. The photo radiates youthful wholesomeness. The dark, piercing eyes stare out in apparent innocence. Everything about the colorful image of Jay Adams belies the fact that he is dead. It makes no sense. Or does it?

I listen intently as the ashen-faced, grieving mother continues the sordid last chapter of her son's story. She tells me how Jay did something seemingly out of character. On a fateful Thursday in September, he purchased a dime bag of marijuana and boasted to his best friend Steve that he was going to sell it. Steve begged him not to. Early on Friday, Jay arrived at school with nine marijuana cigarettes he had rolled by hand. By morning's end, he sold four joints. But Jay had no idea that someone "narked" on him even before the first sale. As he sat in his fifth-hour class, a secretary's voice blared over the intercom, "Please send Jay Adams to the office."

Of course, no one knows what thoughts were in Jay's mind as he walked through the halls of Hanaford High School on his way to that ominous meeting. Most puzzling of all is why he didn't discard the five joints remaining in his pocket. Chances are Jay was deceived into believing his flawless academic standing would protect him.

The assistant principal interrogated Jay, searched him, and found the dope. He had no alternative but to fulfill his responsibility and call the local police. In Hanaford, as in most cities, that is standard procedure when dealing with a case of narcotics possession. The authorities were on the scene within a few minutes. Jay's stepfather, who had been contacted by the school office, arrived as the police officer handcuffed Jay and led him out to the patrol car. Irate yet saddened, the stepfather followed in his own car on the way to the police station. After completing a maze of paperwork and answering what seemed an interminable list of questions, Jay was detained on the narcotics charge. A short time later, he was released to the custody of his dad. Jay was also notified that he had received a five-day suspension from school.

Her voice choking with emotion, Mrs. Adams then described the confrontation at home Friday night. She refers to it as a "four-hour, knock-down-drag-out argument in the living room." It ended with Jay's crying on his parent's shoulders saying, "I'm sorry. I'm sorry. I made a big mistake. It won't happen again." And, he was sincere.

And ill-fitting smile breaks the sullenness of Mrs. Adam's expression as she relives the experience for us. She tells us how satisfied she felt when they hugged and Jay apologized. As he rambled down the basement steps to his bedroom they affectionately called "The Pitt," she was relieved that everything was settled. Jay had failed, but he faced up to his mistakes. He appeared remorseful. Mr. and Mrs. Adams left for their job, early the following Saturday morning. After work, they planned to grill some steaks and put the whole chaotic episode behind them.

Jay's mother told me about her positive feelings as she pulled into the driveway about 3:00 p.m. that afternoon after having bought the groceries for the promised cookout.

In a sense it would be a celebration of family togetherness – Jay had made a dumb decision but in a strange almost inexplicable way it drew them all closer together. Mrs. Adam's fondly remembered how Jay's stepdad, upon his contrition, pledged to go see the principal the high school in an attempt to get him re-enrolled earlier than the penal time allocation. There was a sense of optimism that helped overcome the disgrace and embarrassment of Jay's arrest and suspension from school. Knowing that Jay would be home, she took her car keys from the ignition and dropped them in her purse. Of course, the front door would be unlocked—Jay was grounded, and suspended. Mrs. Adams reached to turn the doorknob and it was locked. Struggling momentarily with that stubborn doorknob, she became instantly angry, thinking Jay was taking advantage of their forgiveness and violating the grounding he was given. Cursing in disgust, Mrs. Adams fished for her keys and unlocked the front door. The slight movement of air caused by the opening of the door rustled a piece of paper strategically placed in the entryway of the floor. At first glance to Mrs. Adams she recognized it was Jay's sloppy handwriting. A she reached down to pick it up; her body was jolted by the words:

Mom,

Don't go downstairs. I've killed myself.

Jay

Mrs. Adams ran down the stairs and into Jay's bedroom. He was sprawled across the bed, bleeding profusely from a bullet wound to the head. At that moment, Jay was alive by a slight heartbeat. If he lived, as many attempters do, he would have been a vegetable in a wheel chair. She searched anxiously for some sign of life, convinced that somehow Jay might survive. Then, in a state of hysteria, Mrs. Adams rushed up the stairs and bolted through the front door. Berserk, screaming in a frenzy of panic and fear, she cried in anguish.

Not one neighbor seemed to hear her or move in her direction. Suddenly, reality confronted her. Momentarily, coming to her senses, Mrs. Adams called the emergency number, 911, and shouted her plea for help. Within moments a paramedic unit was speeding to the house.

Clutching a tissue in her hands, slowly tearing it shreds, Mrs. Adams told me the thoughts that bombarded her brain: Maybe, just maybe, Jay will survive? Please God! If he lives, will he be paralyzed? Will he be mentally demented? Is he going to need to be institutionalized?

Disoriented, her fingers numb, Mrs. Adams managed after several attempts to get a call through on her husband's work phone. Hearing the unbelievable news, Robert ran from the office and leaped into his truck. His heart pounding and his eyes welling with tears, he sped home.

Waiting for the arrival of the emergency team and her husband, Mrs. Adams struggled to maintain some sense of sanity. The stairway to Jay's room seemed to her "a passageway to terror." Her eyes were earnest as she tells me, "There was a dark creeping fear to take even one step down those stairs. Similar to the Mrs. Stoufer's remark after the suicide of her son, it was like some tingling evil presence was waiting for me." Trembling with paranoia in that awful moment, she felt that house had a chilling effect. She called it "a demonic coldness."

The paramedics found Mrs. Adams in Jay's bedroom, bewildered, huddled in the corner in shock. Pushing past her, they began to work feverishly on Jay. Their efforts proved to be futile. Lying on the bed next to Jay's limp body were several bloodstained suicide notes. They give some clue to the mystery of a teenager's life-ending decision.

To the two classmates who sold Jay the dime bag of weed and possibly reported him to the assistant principal to mess us his academic standing, Jay wrote:

Jason, Duane,

You dumb _____ _____. If I said anything you would get me hurt, huh Duane? Well, I've talked and you'll be away for a good period of time. I was quitting. Did you nark? Of course you did. I wrote a letter to the police.

See You in Hell,

Jay

As he indicated, there was another note, addressed to the police. To his older brother, living away from home, Jay left this final message:

Bruce,

What a fine time for me to decide to write a letter. I Thought I'd write you. Take care of Mom and Robert. You all thought I was stronger than what I am.

Love you,

Jay

He reserved the most gripping words for his mother and his stepfather, Robert. Mrs. Adam handed me the crinkled note:

Dear Mom and Robert,

I am sorry for what I put you through. I am empty. I just can't face my friends. I want the entire 9th Grade invited to my funeral. And at the funeral, not before, play this tape. Please don't play it before, if you love me. Also, have Tommy fly down if at all possible. Love you. I'm scared!

Jay

P.S. The tape is in the radio.

P.P.S. Play it at the funeral.

As I finish reading the note, I am deeply sorrowful. Before I can say anything to comfort this bereaved mother, Mrs.

Adams says, "Jerry, the police just released Jay's taped message to me yesterday. They withheld it as evidence until everything was finalized." She continued, "The first time I heard this I was in shock. So this is really my first time to coherently listen to it. I want you to listen to it with me." Almost without hesitation I agree to her request. Since then, I have had second thoughts about that decision.

"I'll be fine," she reassures me. "I'm stronger now." But within seconds after the recording begins, Mrs. Adams loses control. Every word from Jay's clear, pleasant voice is like a dagger to her heart. He is intelligent, articulate, but getting closer to the edge with each statement. Trying to maintain calm, I feel the tears pooling in my eyes, ready to plunge down my cheeks. I am beginning to feel very nervous.

The recording continues, and Mrs. Adams is now frightening me. Though I have been through hundreds of counseling sessions and have dealt with some highly volatile situations, this one is spooking me in a strange way. Jay's mother begins to twist in her chair, in a sort of slow-motion gyration. She groaned and yelped occasionally as if struck by an invisible object. Her eyes pleaded with me, asking, "Why … why … why?"

The last recorded words of Jay Adams ends abruptly. His final words, "Good-bye Mom," echo momentarily, and then there is nothing. Reliving the timeline, I knew this is when he reached for a gun.

The stretcher that carried Jay's wounded body slammed through the emergency room doors at Hanaford Medical Center. But hope was gone. Technically, Jay Adams died of acute blood loss and trauma, and the death certificate indicated a self-inflicted gunshot wound to the head.

Only two hundred mourners attended Jay's funeral. Contrary to Jay's wishes, the recording was not played. It would have caused greater grief, of course. And it not have answered the question every person present was grappling to understand. Why suicide? Jason and Duane did not attend Jay's funeral.

I told one news reporter, "Teenagers tell me three things: Jerry, how do I reach a friend that is into drugs, or abusing alcohol, and thinking about suicide, and many times, that 'friend' is them." If it is not a first-person inquiry, I can, assuredly, tell you that as a friend you might be the only chord of hope to your buddy or girlfriend. Don't sit back and do nothing when you see your friend spiraling down. If there is someone you know in trouble, reach out to him or her. Every minute counts. I meet so many students who do not have a dad at home. I wonder what would have happened to me if I didn't have a dad to call the day I was intent on killing myself. Equally concerning, I meet lots of young people who have parents who don't really care. Scores of times I have listened in disbelief as kids have said to me, "Jerry, I don't do drugs, my parents do!" In our topsy-turvy world, some kids are parents, and some parents are kids. Maybe that is why my school assemblies have been received with such rapt attention. One friend said to me, "You are a father's voice to many kids who don't have one."

CHAPTER 14

Why Not Suicide?

The saddest thing about suicide is that
a person's potential is lost forever.

Ⅰn this book I have tried to share my truest, and most
sincere feelings with you. I know it is a message that
must be shared. A message of life. A message of hope. A
message for you, because you matter.

Maybe you are one of the thousands of teenagers or adults
who have struggled with end-it-all thoughts. Perhaps you've
even tried to take your life, but not completed suicide. Thank
God for that! And, of course, it is possible you have never
thought about suicide at all. At some point you may, and you
need to be prepared to handle it.

There are some really good reasons why you should not
take your own life. For one, no suicide method is foolproof.
Oh, you think you have one that can't miss? Why don't you
talk to the young man who put a gun under his chin, as I
wrote about earlier. The blast removed practically his entire
face, *and he survived*. His girlfriend wrote to tell me the story.
And, I must say it is not the only case I have seen up close. The
morale of that story: when Tony came to consciousness and
saw what he had done, his suicidal thoughts were over, all he
wanted to do was live even if it meant years of reconstructive,

plastic surgery! Some young people of failed suicide attempts are left in nursing homes and institutionalized. With the greatest sadness I have watched their limbs curl in a paralyzed state. Hour after hour they lay there. It is all so unspeakably tragic, but preventable. Every suicide is preventable.

Suppose you do die by suicide. Do you want to be guilty of murder also? How is that possible, you ask? Chances are, you will prompt somebody near you to think about completing suicide just because you have, and maybe, just maybe, that person will also die by suicide. We refer to this as the *contagion effect*. It is very common that family members, i.e., mom, dad, brother, or sister, and close friends later attempt suicide when someone close to them, who they love, dies by suicide. You don't want to do that to your mom or dad, brother or sister, do you? It has happened hundreds of times before. You have family and friends and have no guarantee that they will be the exception.

When someone dies by suicide, it is final. Maybe that sounds insultingly elementary. I mention it only because so many teenagers I've talked to have mistakenly thought that suicide is temporary, that somehow they are going to come back like the actor who dies in one movie and lives again in another. It doesn't work that way. Again, suicide is a *permanent solution to temporary problems*. Whatever is really bugging you today, chances are you will not even remember it six months from now. Is that worth killing yourself? I have found in my own life that my toughest adversities and problems, as difficult as they were to endure, truly have shaped me to be a better, more caring person. Down deep, I know God is working a mysterious plan for my life, even when I do not understand it. He is doing the same in your life. Someone said, "When we cannot trace God's hand in our life, we can always trust His heart." I agree, and have lived long enough to know with certainty that it is true.

Like the parents of Aaron Stoufer, Jay Adams, and Don

Simmonds' star hockey player, Dylan, the survivors are *never* the same. If you kill yourself, you will drastically change the lives of others who love you. There are people who care deeply about you that you are not even aware of. You will ruin their lives, but you will be the biggest loser.

The saddest thing about suicide is that a person's potential is *lost forever.* And his or her purpose is snuffed out as crudely as a boot heel crushing a cigarette butt. Kill yourself, and you will stop dreams from coming true. Do you really want it to end that way?

Remember, your problems are temporary. They may seem like a storm that will never pass, but the rains *will stop,* the sky will clear, the clouds will drift away, and the sunshine *will* reappear. If you break up with somebody, you may feel that your whole world has caved in and that nothing will ever be the same. I remember those feelings very well, and the hurt does run deep. But, it *does* go away, and it's sure not worth ending your life.

Don't ever make a big decision when you are discouraged or under stress. If depressive thoughts linger in your mind and you can't seem to get rid of them, set up a counseling appointment with a good pastor, or a mental health therapist, call our Prayer Line, 1-866-273-4444, at Crossroads, or call the Suicide Prevention hotline, 1-800-273-TALK (8255), first before trying to take your life. Give a reputable counselor a chance. I doubt that anyone ever committed suicide when not under some kind of stress *and* when they were not giving a qualified counselor an opportunity to thoughtfully help them work through the difficulties.

Please, please get rid of any glamorous idea you might have of suicide. Suicide is not glamorous. The media has taken the advice from the leading suicidologists of North America and rarely now even cover adolescent or adult suicides. They learned from experts that dramatic stories and pictures in newspapers and magazines only contributed to the contagion effect. With the exception of celebrities, most teenage and adult suicides are all but ignored in the media. And this was a smart move. Again, there is nothing glamorous about suicide. If you take a bunch of pills, you won't just drift off into an eternal sleep. Quite frequently heavy doses of medication induce vomiting, which in some instances, prevents suicide. As you die, your sphincter muscles will relax and your excrement will come out and make you an ugly sight indeed. If you shoot yourself, who is going to clean up the mess? Somebody has to do it.

Let me also tell you about your accountability to God and eternity. I have said it so many times, "Only God gives life, and only God should take it." Suicide is self-murder and it breaks one of the Ten Commandments, "Thou shalt not kill." Also, the minute a person dies, he or she continues to live, either in heaven or hell. There is no annihilation or extinction of the soul. Give some serious thought to your responsibility before God.

There is hope. There are so many people who do care. Turn to them in your time of greatest tension. Talk to someone you trust who can give you wise counsel. If you feel like you don't have anyone else, or you feel a special connection with me, then write to me. If you want me to come speak to the students in your area, write to me.

Why not suicide? You are the answer to that question. Your life is too valuable, too meaningful, too promising. Choose life.

Can I share with you what I would have missed had I killed myself in that family room of my dad's home as a teenager? Forgive me for being personal, but there is something in me that makes me think you might want to know. You see every young person who dies by suicide misses so much. Life has challenges, but life is filled with so many joys and experiences.

Had I completed suicide on Friday, April 13, 1973, I would have never met the girl of my dreams, Cristie Jo Huf, just five years later. I was speaking in Holland, Michigan. After a year of excellent grades at the Lou Rog School of Hair Design, the state board informed Cristie she had failed her final exam. She was so distraught; she came to the event where I was speaking with her dad. The last night of a three-week campaign, the Huf family invited me to hang out at their home. We have been hanging out ever since—34 incredible years. (By the way, Cristie did not fail her exam—it was a clerical error, just in the nick of time to motivate her to go to the crusade where I was speaking! Only God, right?)

Imagining my life, without the love of my life, seems impossible. Cristie has brought me such immense joy. To this very day, I believe she is the most beautiful woman I have ever seen. I tell her all the time, "You are filled with such goodness." We would have never consummated our love—something that never gets old, and only gets better. I would not have been able to experience the inexpressible thrill of watching Danielle, Jeremy, and Jenilee, our three dynamic children, birthed into this world. I would have never discovered that Cristie would become my very closest friend. How many amazing nights we have had together … tender moments sharing our hearts with one another … always encouraging one another. Suicide would have robbed me of Cristie.

I would have never experienced the unspeakable joy and pride of being a father. Danielle, my firstborn, was a blond-haired little angel. I use to tuck her into bed almost every night when I was home, sit by her bedside, hold her little hand, and prayed many a prayer with her. And, I would have been deprived of leading her to Christ in Chattanooga, Tennessee, when she would not go to bed without inviting Jesus into her heart. We would have never been able to take that unforgettable trip to New York City, when I was on the Sally Jessy Raphael TV Show, and the crowd was beating up on me until she stood and spoke in my defense. I remember her leaning against my shoulder, and me keeping her warm, during the *Phantom of the Opera* that night at the Majestic Theatre. I would not have been able to lead her down the aisle and simultaneously officiate at her gorgeous wedding had I died by suicide. Blessed with her two children, Kasey Marie and little Christian—I can't even begin to fathom not being a grandfather because it is a whole lot of fun spoiling grandchildren!

I would have missed the stunning pride of having a son, Jeremiah Jay, now soon to finish his Ph.D. from Oxford, England! He is a superb communicator and Christian apologist. His social skills are off the charts. Jeremy became my best friend when he was five-years-old, and has traveled all over the world with me. He came to Christ in my crusade at Jimmy Draper's church in Euless, Texas. My road assistant walked Jeremy down the aisle on his shoulders and I can remember that little guy waving at me as if to say, "Dad, I am deciding for Christ tonight." In Davis, Oklahoma, at a youth camp with 5,000 campers in attendance, Jeremy came forward again and dedicated his life to Christian ministry. A photographer snapped a picture of me leaning down from the platform, my arms around his neck, praying with him. Wow! What memories! Jeremy has stood loyally and faithfully at my side. We talk so many times on the phone each day and rarely does he ever hang up without saying, "Dad, I love you." His wife, Audrey, and their two exceptional children, Lily Faith, and Justin Jay, are priceless gifts in my life. Just looking at their pictures on my iPhone, all my problems vanish and strength surges into my being. Suicide would have prevented me from having a son who makes me so proud.

Jenilee Nicole, my second daughter, came along in 1985. Talk about a girl who makes her dad so proud. She was straight as an arrow growing up. Jeni's always had such a heart for God. During a trip to South Africa, a baby with AIDS bit Jeni on the hand deep enough to draw blood. Upon her return home, the doctor asked her and her husband to refrain from trying to have a baby for six month to a year. At the time, it is disappointing and frightful. After repeated testing over the course of many months, Jeni was negative with the HIV virus. Sadly, it was later revealed her husband was having an affair with a teen in our church's youth group. Her marriage ended in divorce and Jeni came home to live with us. She endured torturous months of loneliness. I went with her to a divorce attorney, something we both thought would never happen, and something that has given us such a large heart for men and women who experience the trauma of divorce. She would curl her legs up next to her body on the couch in my home study, and in shock stare at me with those big eyes and ask, "Dad, am I going to be okay?" Without hesitation, I one night I replied, "Oh, Jeni, God has such a wonderful plan for your life. Just watch what the Lord does. You are going to be married one year from now." I don't know why I said it. No dad could make such a promise. A cultured, incredibly softhearted, strong young man, Jeffrey Vance Mullikin, later came into her life and they fell madly in love. Just before I walked down the makeshift aisle on a beach in Ft. Lauderdale, Florida, where she was wed, Jenilee turned to me and said, "Dad, do you remember what you told me?"

I said, "What honey?"

She returned, "You told me a one year ago that I would be remarried and happy. Dad, thanks for being there."

Tears just welled up in my eyes. She looked so beautiful. I gently took her hand and said, "Let's go." Suicide would have taken all of these wonderful memories away. That is why when we are depressed, and filled with hopelessness, we don't give up. We reach out, instead of withdrawing in. *There is hope!*

Finally, suicide would have prevented me from reaching thousands upon thousands of young people and adults all over the world. How many exactly? I don't know. God does. It is a lot of people. One young mother in her early twenties came to hear me speak. After my talk, she came up to me and tried to speak but could not articulate her words. Tears rolled down her pretty cheeks as she was holding a picture of two little cute kids. They were her children.

Slowly, and purposefully, she said, "Jerry, you came to my high school and spoke. I was going to kill myself. Because you came, I received help. If you wouldn't have come, my two children would have never been born. Thank you … thank you … thank you," she reiterated. It was one of the moments where you really know why you are alive, and realize there is no greater feeling than helping someone in need.

I have given you plenty of reasons *not* to kill yourself. But, there is one more reason … a step you must take, and I can guarantee you, if you do, you will not be thinking about suicide again. I have saved the best for last. It's in the next chapter, read on.

Why Not Suicide?

CHAPTER 15

How To Start All Over

Standing right next to me, Cindy asked, "Jerry, do you know
Jesus?" I couldn't believe her interest in me.
Did she know I was almost dead eleven weeks earlier?

Do you remember my story that began this book in Chapter 1? I was at the end of my rope hanging on for dear life and my parents bribed me to go to a summer youth camp by promising me a professional foosball table for my birthday. I had never been to a camp, let alone a *Christian* camp. It sounded like going to a monastery to me at the time.

Windermere camp had two meetings each day, one in the morning and one at night. Hundreds of young people filled the long, narrow auditorium, and they began each meeting singing songs that I have never heard of. I attended only one of the morning services and the speaker was unusually boring. I had no idea what he was talking about, so I cut out. During the morning "chapel" time the remainder of the week I roamed about Windermere's lakeside resort.

On the last night of camp, Thursday night, June 21, I found myself seated on the back row anticipating leaving camp the next day and going back to party with my friends. Unbeknownst to me, a group of young people had been praying for me all week and had gone to the camp speaker and asked him to do the same.

At the time my family was a wreck. My Mom was an alcoholic. My poor Dad was on the verge of a heart attack mediating five sons, and knowing that I, in particular, was on the verge of suicide. My older brother, Jeff, had run away from home and met a junkie and hitched trains to California. That guy turned him on to some heavy drugs. Jeff was being pushed down a four-lane highway in a shopping cart, high, in the state of California, when the police picked him up. My Mom had flown out to get him and bring him back home. Life was tough and uncertain for the Johnston family.

Just before the camp speaker began his final night's talk, I noticed a beautiful girl, Cindy, grade eleven. I had admired her beauty all week, and she was walking down the aisle and heading straight for me. Awesome, I thought!

Cindy stuck out her delicate hand and said, "Jerry, why don't you come up and sit with me tonight. I want you to hear what the speaker has to say."

I didn't care about the speaker, or his talk, but under my breath as I sprang out of my seat I said, "Wherever you lead, *I will follow!*"

It was a little peculiar on that second row. I had never sat near the front before. The speaker seemed so close and for once I decided to listen. Bob shared how God loved each and every person. In fact, Bob said, God demonstrated His love by sending Jesus Christ to live, die, and rise again from the dead so that He could forgive the sin of *anyone* who would come to Him by faith and invite Him into their heart and life.

I had never heard that message before. Our posh Johnson County church was such a turn off that I never listened. My brothers and I use to have candle fights at the Christmas Eve services and see if we could light one another on fire.

That night at camp I realized that I had never invited

Jesus Christ into my life. No wonder I was so empty...so filled with despair, always searching for something to fill the emptiness in my heart. The camp speaker quoted John 3:16, "For God so loved the world that He gave His only begotten Son, that whoever believes in Him should not perish but have everlasting life." Bob made it clear. You don't go to heaven by just attending church or being a good person. You have to receive Jesus Christ into your heart. You have to invite Him into your life.

At the end of his talk, the camp speaker invited everyone in the audience who wanted to receive Christ to come forward. Music was playing and my heart was pounding. For the first time in my life it was as if God was speaking directly to me.

Standing right next to me, Cindy asked, "Jerry, do you know Jesus?" I couldn't believe her interest in me. Did she know I was almost dead eleven weeks earlier?

God helping me, I left my seat and walked to the front. That night I prayed a prayer that changed my life and began my new life with Christ. Would you pray this prayer with me, too?

Dear God,

Thank you for sending Jesus Christ to die on the cross paying the price for my sin. I believe Jesus rose from the dead. Right now, by faith, I invite Jesus to come into my heart and please forgive me of my sins. Thank you that I am forgiven, and am now Your child.

In Jesus' Name,

Amen

In an instant, and internally, I knew something happened at that very moment! Christ had come into my heart. I had become a Christian, and, man oh man, did it feel so good. Later that night, I found the camp speaker, Bob, at his room and told him my whole story. He encouraged me to go home and *live for God*. Bob told me to tell my parents and friends that I was a new person ... a child of God.

I could not wait to get home. An older friend at camp had a Camaro. I jumped in and we drove nearly 100 miles an hour on the way home so I could tell my mom and dad that I was a "new Jerry." When I entered the front door of our suburbia home I hollered as loud as I could, "Mom and Dad, I am home. Come down here I have to tell you something." My Dad was startled, wondering what I was up to now. Quickly they assembled themselves in our family room.

"Dad, Mom, I am Christian! Jesus Christ lives in my heart! Everything is brand new. The emptiness is gone! I don't want to do drugs anymore," I told them.

Mom started crying. Dad did too. I could tell something brand new was beginning in our home that very moment. Darkness was leaving and the light of Christ was illuminating every inch of our home.

That first Sunday, the pastor of Teresa's church shelved his sermon and invited the youth who had gone to camp to come share a testimony in the Sunday morning service. I had never heard of that word "testimony." In anticipation, the night before, I had my Mom iron a shirt and get me a sport coat and slacks to wear, instead of those jeans I used to live in and get high in. Sunday morning I had my dad tie a red bow tie on me!

After a few teenagers shared, I left my seat and climbed the stairs of the church platform and shared with the entire congregation how Jesus Christ changed my life and how I was going to share Jesus with everyone I knew! Mom and dad were crying. Both of them came forward that morning and gave their hearts to Jesus Christ.

I started a Youth for Christ club for my school and in one year we led over 200 of our classmates to faith in Christ.

It was my job every Monday night at the YFC Club to give the invitation for teens to receive Christ. I so fell in love with seeing people coming to Christ that I have been sharing the Gospel every since.

If you have never received Christ, let me urge you to pray the same prayer I did. And when you do, write me or call our Prayer Line at 1-866-273-4444 and tell one of our advisors you prayed to receive Jesus Christ. Walk with God. Read the Bible. Grow in your relationship with Christ. The Christian walk is not a bed of roses, but you will never walk alone again, and you will never face any of your problems alone again.

Crossroads Centre
Prayer Lines

Depressed? Feel all alone? Do you need to talk to someone? We are waiting, 24/7. The call is free.

1-866-273-4444

www.crossroads.ca

Since the very first broadcast of *100 Huntley Street* on June 15, 1977 the Prayer Lines have played a key role in what takes place through Crossroads as instant two-way communication made immediate response possible. From that first program where people called to receive Jesus Christ as their Savior and Lord, follow-up was an important and integral part of this ministry. Follow-up then became follow through in connecting these precious people to caring churches throughout the nation. Now over 35 years later with millions of calls received and thousands of salvation decisions for Jesus Christ recorded, the immediacy of response continues through the phone line. Now Internet access to our Crossroads website opens a whole new realm of contact worldwide!

In the Crossroads Prayer Ministry, desperate, broken and suicidal people find the hope and help they so crave. Here they are introduced to the reality that "the Lord is close to the brokenhearted and saves those who are crushed in spirit." *(Psalm 34:18)* Rather than being told God is far from them because they are broken, just the opposite is true. His Word declares He is "close to the brokenhearted," and that is liberation, an invitation to draw near this caring Lord! Here in the Crossroads Prayer Centre we have come to understand that Jesus is the "wounded healer" *(Isaiah 53:5)* who comes to us in our own woundedness. Amazingly, as we allow His woundedness to touch ours, healing takes place. Over time, and as we give him permission to work in our lives, we then become "wounded healers" to others through the very grace and healing we have received from Jesus! The invitation of Jesus in Matthew 11:28-30 is one we continually declare through the Prayer Centre to our broken world: *"Come to me, all you who are weary and burdened, and I will give you rest. Take my yoke upon you and learn from me, for I am gentle and humble in heart, and you will find rest for your souls. For my yoke is easy and my burden is light."* The Message says it like this: "Are you tired? Worn out? Burned out on religion? Come to me. Get away with me and you'll recover your life. I'll show you how to take a real rest. Walk with me and work with me—watch how I do it. Learn the unforced rhythms of grace. I won't lay anything heavy or ill-fitting on you. Keep company with me and you'll learn to live freely and lightly."

Have you come to Him? If not, allow your brokenness to be the key in allowing you to discover. He is near. We are waiting to love and help you.

End Notes

[a] Dobson, Dr. James. *Children At Risk*. Thomas Nelson, 1994.

[1] "Mental Health—Depression," Health Canada: www.hc-sc. gc.ca/hl-vs/iyh-vsv/diseases-maladies/depression-eng.php#ba (accessed August 22, 2012).

[2] *"Improving Early Identification & Treatment of Adolescent Depression: Considerations & Strategies for Health Plans,"* NIHCM Foundation Issue Brief, February 2010. http:// nihcm.org/pdf/Adol_MH_Issue_Brief_Final.pdf (access August 22, 2012).

[3] Tim LaHaye, *How to Win Over Depression* (Grand Rapids, MI: Zondervan, 1979), 24.

[4] Dan Elliott and Nicholas Riccardi, "James Holmes, Aurora Shooting Suspect, Made Threats Months Before 'Dark Knight' Massacre, Prosecutors Say." *Huffington Post*, August 24, 2012: www.huffingtonpost.com/2012/08/24/James-holmes-threats-aurora-colorado_n_1828616.html (accessed August 25, 2012).

[5] Peter Langman, "Dylan Kelbold's Journal and Other Writings," www.schoolshooters.info/dylan-klebold-journal. pdf (accessed August 22, 2012).

[6] Susan Klebold, "I Will Never Know Why," *Oprah Magazine*, November, 2009. www.oprah.com/world/Susan-Klebolds-O-Magazine-Essay-I-Will-Never-Know-Why/1 (accessed August 22, 2012).

[7] "Basement Tapes" March 15, 1999, Evidence item #265, http://acolumbinesite.com/quotes1.html (accessed August 22, 2012).

[8] "Youth Suicidal Behavior—Fact Sheet," *American Association of Suicidology:* www.suicidology.org/c/ document_library/get_file?folderId=248&name=DLFE-416.

pdf (accessed August 23, 2012).

[9] Web-based Injury Statistics Query and Reporting System (WISQARS), 2010. *Centers for Disease Control and Prevention (CDC):* www.cdc.gov/injury/wisqars/index.html (accessed August 21, 2012).

[10] David Shaffer, *Teenage Suicide.* National Alliance of Mental Illness, www.nami.org/Content/ContentGroups/Helpline1/Teenage_Suicide.htm (accessed August 23, 2012).

[11] SK Goldsmith, TC Pellmar, AM Kleinman, WE Bunney, editors. *Reducing Suicide: a national imperative.* Washington, DC: National Academy Press, 2002.

[12] About Suicide, Canadian Association for Suicide Prevention. www.suicideprevention.ca/about-suicide/ (accessed August 20, 2012).

[13] "Suicide rates: An overview," in Health at a Glance, www.statcan.gc.ca/pub/82-624-x/2012001/article/11696-eng.htm (accessed August 20, 2012).

[14] Marcia Seligson, "Are You Suicidal?" *Harper's Bazaar* (August 1972), 63.

[15] N. L. Farberow, Some Facts About Suicide (Washington, D.C.: U. S. Government Printing Office, 1961), 12.

[16] "Suicide in the U.S.: Statistics and Prevention," *The National Institute of Mental Health*, www.nimh.nih.gov/health/publications/suicide-in-the-us-statistics-and-prevention/index (access August 20, 2012).

[17] Pamela Cantor, "Schools Must Help These Tragedies," *USA Today,* Feb 26, 1986, (accessed Sept 5, 2012).

[18] Giovanna Breu, "When Hopelessness Sets In, Warns Psychiatrist Aaron Beck, Suicide Can Be Close Behind," *People* (April 7, 1986), 93.

[19] Ibid., 93-94.

[20] Miller, Larry. "Life As A Rock Star Can Kill You." *CBS News Entertainment*, February 11, 2009. www.cbsnews.. com/2100-207_162-3230264.html (accessed August 26, 2012).

[21] Cynthia Taylor, "Helping the Suicidal," *Eternity* (March 1985), 32.

[22] Ibid, 33.

[23] Robert J. Barry, "Teenage Suicide: An American Tragedy," *FBI Law Enforcement Bulletin* (April 1986), 17.

[24] William Steele, "Preventing the Spread of Suicide Among Adolescents," *USA Today Magazine* (November 1985), 59.

[25] Taylor, 32.

[26] "Nightline," *ABC Network* (November 1984).

[27] Steven Stack, "A Leveling Off in Young Suicide," *The Wall Street Journal* (May 28, 1986), 34.

[28] George Howard Colt, "The Enigma of Suicide," Harvard Magazine, Sept-Oct 1983), 47-48.

[29] Jacoba Urist, "Sex in Movies Pushes Kids To Have Sex Earlier," Forbes, www.forbes.com/sites/ jacobaurist/2012/08/08/sex-in-movies-pushes-kids-to-have-sex-earlier/ (accessed September 4, 2012).

[30] "The Games Teenagers Play," *Newsweek* (September 1, 19080), 49.

[31] "Sexual Intercourse," *Youth Risk Behavior Surveillance.* The U.S. Center for Disease Control and Prevention, www. sexedlibrary.org/index.cfm?pageId=815 (accessed September 4, 2012).

[32] Claudia Wallis, "Children Having Children," *Time* (December 9, 1985), 82.

[33] Christine Langlois, "Teen Sexuality," *Canadian Living,* www.canadianliving.com/moms/family_life/teen_sexuality.

php (accessed September 4, 2012).

[34] Sally Helms and Robert Tenenbaum, "Kids and Sex," *Columbus Monthly* (November 1981), 58-66.

[35] Susan Donaldson James, "Auto-Erotic Asphyxia's Deadly Thrill," *ABC News*, June 5, 2009, http://abcnews.go.com/Health/story?id=7764618&page=1#.UEaADkI28lI (accessed September 4, 2012).

[36] "Alcohol causes 2.5 million death a year: WHO." *CBC News*, February 11, 2011, www.cbc.ca/news/health/story/2011/02/11/health-alcohol-deaths.html (accessed September 4, 2012).

[37] "CDC report shows about 112 million annual incidents of people drinking and driving Centers," *U.S. Center for Disease Control and Prevention*, October 2011, www.cdc.gov/media/releases/2011/p1004_drinking_driving.html (accessed September 4, 2012).

[38] "Teen Drivers: Fact Sheet." Centers for Disease Control and Prevention, www.cdc.gov/motorvehiclesafety/teen_drivers/teendrivers_factsheet.html (accessed September 4, 2012).

[39] "Alcohol Addiction," www.alcoholaddiction.info/alcoholism-statistics.htm (accessed September 4, 2012).

[40] Used by students Grades 7-12 In the past year. Angela Paglia-Boak, Robert E. Mann, Edward M. Adlaf, Jürgen Rehm, *Drug Use Among Ontario Students 2009 Study* (CAMH), http://goo.gl/Travy.

[41] Ibid.

[42] "Substance Use by Canadian Youth - A National Survey of Canadians' Use of Alcohol and Other Drugs - Canadian Addiction Survey," Health Canada, http://goo.gl/PTQve (accessed Sept 5, 2012).

[43] Sources: U.S. = *National Institute on Drug Abuse; Canada = Centre for Addiction and Mental Health & Canadian*

Centre on Substance Abuse (2004).

[44] Ibid.

[45] Alan Duke and Saeed Ahmed, "More associates link Jackson to prescription drugs," *CNN*, July 8, 2009.

[46] Syvia Hui, "Amy Winehouse Autopsy: Coroner Says Singer Died From Too Much Alcohol," *HuffPost Celebrity Canada*, www.huffingtonpost.com/2011/10/26/amy-winehouse-dead-singer-alcohol_n_1032344.html (accessed September 5, 2012).

[47] "Lost Girl: The Fierce Life and Tortured Times of Amy Winehouse," *Q Magazine*, August 2012, 85.

[48] Peggy Mann, *Marijuana Alert* (New York: McGraw-Hill, 1985), 18-19.

[49] Weekly Reader (January 7-21, 1986) 1.

[50] "Survey Shows Drug-Infested US High Schools," *The Fix*, www.thefix.com/content/drugs-us-high-schools90497 (accessed September 5, 2012).

[51] Bob Meehan with Stephen J. Meyer, "Is Your Child Taking Drugs?" *Reader's Digest* (July 1986), 57.

*photo credit: Kansas City Star.

Bibliography

BOOKS

Goldsmith, SK, TC Pellmar, AM Kleinman, WE Bunney, eds. *Reducing Suicide: a national imperative.* Washington, DC: National Academy Press, 2002.

Farberow, N. L. *Some Facts About Suicide.* Washington, D.C.: U. S. Government Printing Office, 1961.

Mann, Peggy. *Marijuana Alert.* New York: McGraw-Hill, 1985.

LaHaye, Tim. *How to Win Over Depression.* Grand Rapids, MI: Zondervan, 1979.

ARTICLES

Barry, Robert J. "Teenage Suicide: An American Tragedy." *FBI Law Enforcement Bulletin,* April 1986.

Breu, Giovanna. "When Hopelessness Sets In, Warns Psychiatrist Aaron Beck, Suicide Can Be Close Behind." *People,* April 7, 1986.

Cantor, Pamela. "Schools Must Help These Tragedies." *USA Today,* Feb 26, 1986. Accessed Sept 5, 2012.

Colt, George Howard. "The Enigma of Suicide." *Harvard Magazine*, Sept-Oct 1983.

Duke, Alan and Saeed Ahmed. "More associates link Jackson to prescription drugs." *CNN*, July 8, 2009.

Elliott, Dan and Nicholas Riccardi. "James Holmes, Aurora Shooting Suspect, Made Threats Months Before 'Dark Knight' Massacre, Prosecutors Say." *Huffington Post*, Aug 24, 2012: www.huffingtonpost.com/2012/08/24/James-holmes-threats-aurora-colorado_n_1828616.html (accessed August 25, 2012).

Helms, Sally and Robert Tenenbaum. "Kids and Sex." *Columbus Monthly*, November 1981.

Hui, Syvia. "Amy Winehouse Autopsy: Coroner Says Singer Died From Too Much Alcohol." *HuffPost Celebrity Canada*, www.huffingtonpost.com/2011/10/26/amy-winehouse-dead-singer-alcohol_n_1032344.html (accessed September 5, 2012).

Klebold, Susan. "I Will Never Know Why." *Oprah Magazine*, Nov, 2009. www.oprah.com/world/Susan-Klebolds-O-Magazine-Essay-I-Will-Never-Know-Why/1 (accessed August 22, 2012).

Langlois, Christine. "Teen Sexuality." *Canadian Living*. www.canadianliving.com/moms/family_life/teen_sexuality.php (accessed Sept 4, 2012).

Meehan, Bob with Stephen J. Meyer. "Is Your Child Taking Drugs?" *Reader's Digest*, July 1986.

Miller, Larry. "Life As A Rock Star Can Kill You." *CBS News Entertainment*, Feb 11, 2009. www.cbsnews.com/2100-207_162-3230264.html (accessed August 26, 2012).

Seligson, Marcia. "Are You Suicidal?" *Harper's Bazaar*, August 1972.

Stack, Steven. "A Leveling Off in Young Suicide." *The Wall Street Journal*, May 28, 1986.

Steele, William. "Preventing the Spread of Suicide Among Adolescents." *USA Today Magazine*, November 1985.

Taylor, Cynthia. "Helping the Suicidal." *Eternity*, March 1985.

Urist, Jacoba. "Sex in Movies Pushes Kids To Have Sex Earlier." *Forbes*. www.forbes.com/sites/jacobaurist/2012/08/08/sex-in-movies-pushes-kids-to-have-sex-earlier. Accessed September 4, 2012.

Wallis, Claudia. "Children Having Children," *Time,* December 9, 1985.

"Alcohol causes 2.5 million death a year: WHO." *CBC News,* Feb 11, 2011, www.cbc.ca/news/health/story/2011/02/11/ health-alcohol-deaths.html. Accessed Sept 4, 2012.

"CDC report shows about 112 million annual incidents of people drinking and driving Centers." *U.S. Center for Disease Control and Prevention,* October 2011. www.cdc. gov/media/releases/2011/p1004_drinking_driving.html. Accessed Sept 4, 2012.

"Lost Girl: The Fierce Life and Tortured Times of Amy Winehouse," *Q Magazine,* August 2012, 1985.

"Survey Shows Drug-Infested US High Schools." *The Fix.* www.thefix.com/content/drugs-us-high-schools90497. Accessed September 5, 2012.

"The Games Teenagers Play." *Newsweek,* September 1, 1980.

WEBSITES AND STUDIES

About Suicide, Canadian Association for Suicide Prevention. www.suicideprevention.ca/about-suicide/ (accessed August 20, 2012).

"Alcohol Addiction," www.alcoholaddiction.info/ alcoholism-statistics.htm (accessed Sept 4, 2012). Barna Group of Ventura, California www.barna.org (Research 2008)

"Basement Tapes" March 15, 1999, Evidence item #265, http://acolumbinesite.com/quotes1.html (accessed August 22, 2012).

Centers for Disease Control and Prevention (CDC): www.cdc. gov/injury/wisqars/index.html (accessed August 21, 2012).

"Improving Early Identification & Treatment of Adolescent Depression: Considerations & Strategies for Health Plans," *NIHCM Foundation Issue Brief,* February 2010. http://nihcm. org/pdf/Adol_MH_Issue_Brief_Final.pdf (accessed August 22, 2012).

Langman, Peter. "Dylan Kelbold's Journal and Other Writings." www.schoolshooters.info/dylan-klebold-journal. pdf (accessed August 22, 2012).

"Mental Health – Depression," *Health Canada*: www.hc-sc. gc.ca/hl-vs/iyh-vsv/diseases-maladies/depression-eng.php#ba (accessed August 22, 2012).

"Nightline," *ABC Network* (November 1984).

"Sexual Intercourse," *Youth Risk Behavior Surveillance.* The U.S. Center for Disease Control and Prevention, www. sexedlibrary.org/index.cfm?pageId=815 (accessed September 4, 2012).

Shaffer, David. *Teenage Suicide.* National Alliance of Mental Illness, www.nami.org/Content/ContentGroups/Helpline1/ Teenage_Suicide.htm (accessed August 23, 2012).

"Substance Use by Canadian Youth - A National Survey of Canadians' Use of Alcohol and Other Drugs - Canadian Addiction Survey," *Health Canada*, http://goo.gl/PTQve (accessed Sept 5, 2012).

"Suicide in the U.S.: Statistics and Prevention," *The National Institute of Mental Health,* www.nimh.nih.gov/health/ publications/suicide-in-the-us-statistics-and-prevention/ index (access August 20, 2012).

"Suicide rates: An overview," in *Health at a Glance*, www. statcan.gc.ca/pub/82-624-x/2012001/article/11696-eng.htm (accessed August 20, 2012).

"Teen Drivers: Fact Sheet." *Centers for Disease Control and Prevention*, www.cdc.gov/motorvehiclesafety/teen_drivers/

teendrivers_factsheet.html (accessed Sept 4, 2012).

Paglia-Boak, Angela, Robert E. Mann, Edward M. Adlaf, and Jürgen Rehm. *Drug Use Among Ontario Students 2009 Study* (CAMH), http://goo.gl/Travy.

"Youth Suicidal Behavior – Fact Sheet," *American Association of Suicidology:* www.suicidology.org/c/document_library/get_file?folderld=248&name=DLFE-416.pdf (accessed August 23, 2012).

Dr. Jerry Johnston—Profile

Jerry Johnston (Doctor of Ministry—Acadia University Divinity College, Wolfville, Nova Scotia) has captivated over 4,000,000 youth on more than 2,500 public school campuses, addressing vital issues. He has held events in over 1,200 churches of all denominations throughout the United States and Canada. Over 125,000 people have come to faith in Jesus Christ through his invitation. Jerry has authored 12 books and produced 12 videos that have been distributed to thousands of churches. He has presented 112 different popular teaching series comprised of over 900 expositional messages on video, many of which are available online.

While still in high school, Jerry's ministry career began as an Evangelist-at-Large for Youth for Christ, the same ministry that launched Billy Graham. He received a scholarship to Liberty University, Lynchburg, VA. While there he served as an Associate Evangelist with Dr. Jerry Falwell and was featured on the Old Time Gospel Hour TV and radio networks. Later, Jerry was awarded an Honorary Doctor of Divinity degree by Liberty Baptist Theological Seminary, Lynchburg, Virginia (1997).

Dr. Johnston has extensive media experience and has been interviewed on *Fox News' The O'Reilly Factor, Good Morning America, World News Tonight, Nightline; The Today Show,* CNN's *Crossfire,* Deborah Norville Tonight, MSNBC's Scarborough Country, *Connected Coast to Coast with Ron Reagan, Focus on the Family, The 700 Club, 100 Huntley Street* in Canada, and many others.

Jerry's wife, Dr. Cristie Jo Johnston, is an effective teacher of God's Word who has broad appeal to both men and women. The Johnston's have three children: Danielle, married to Christian Newsome, senior pastor of The Journey Church, Lee's Summit, MO; Jeremiah Johnston, Ph.D. (cand.),

Lecturer in Biblical Studies, Acadia Divinity College, married to Audrey; and Jenilee, married to Jeffrey Mullikin.

Jerry has served as an effective consultant to pastors and various ministries on media development, fundraising, and mentoring leaders.

To schedule Jerry to speak in your church, school, or area write or call:

In Canada:	In the United States:
Crossroads	Crossroads
P.O. Box 5100	P. O. Box 486
1295 North Service Road	Niagara Falls, NY
Burlington, Ontario	14302
L7R 4M2	

905-332-6400, ext. 3231

www.jerryjohnston.com

 Jerry Johnston on Twitter:
twitter.com/Jerry_Johnston

 Jerry Johnston on Facebook:
facebook.com/DrJerryJohnston

Don Simmonds—Profile

As Chairman and CEO, Don brings a blend of experiences in both business and ministry. In a media dominated society, he believes strongly that God's love for people needs to be presented in a relevant way through the power of today's media technology.

Don and his wife Fay have been married for 37 years and live in Uxbridge, Ontario. They have four children. Shauna (29), Craig (26), Brett (25) and April (15). With their love for God and commitment to family as overriding priorities, Don and Fay have enjoyed a full life focused on two of the most rapidly changing environments: the electronics business and the teenage world.

In business Don is known as a *"serial entrepreneur"*, having been involved in over 20 new ventures in the last 30 years. The businesses cover a diverse range of ideas from consumer audio products to solar electric power to dairy farming! Don was one of seven partners that started the Lenbrook Group in 1977, a private business incubation company perhaps best known for having created Clearnet, one of Canada's wireless networks sold in 2001 to Telus.

Don was the founding CEO of AirIQ Inc., a business providing wireless GPS tracking for all types of vehicles and marine vessels. During his years as CEO, AirIQ was named one of Canada's fastest growing technology companies. Don was a finalist in the Ernst & Young Entrepreneur Of The Year® Awards in 2005.

Don and his wife Fay have been youth leaders at their church in Uxbridge for many years. From 1991-1994 Don left the business environment to work more intensely with youth as the National Youth Coordinator for Canadian Baptists and then enjoyed being the Executive Director of Toronto Youth for Christ (now Youth Unlimited). From 1980 to 1990

Don served as Canada's representative to Baptist World Alliance Youth and assisted in the planning of world youth conferences in Argentina, Scotland and Zimbabwe.

Don has been a private pilot, serves on a number of profit and not for profit boards, and particularly appreciates the opportunity to coach the young men on the Uxbridge Tigers High School Hockey team whose motto is *"winning at hockey and winning in life!"*

To schedule Don to speak in your church, school, or area write or call:

Crossroads
P.O. Box 5100
1295 North Service Road
Burlington, Ontario
L7R 4M2

905-332-6400, ext. 3222

For Further Help

American Academy of Child & Adolescent Psychiatry
3615 Wisconsin Ave., NW
Washington, DC 20016-3007
202-966-7300
www.aacap.org

American Association of Suicidology
4201 Connecticut Ave., NW
Washington, DC 20008
202-237-2280
www.suicidology.org

American Foundation for Suicide Prevention
120 Wall Street, 22nd Floor
New York, NY 10005
888-333-AFSP (2377)
www.afsp.org

The Barna Group
2368 Eastman Ave., Unit 12
Ventura, CA 93003
805-639-0000
800-55-BARNA (USA only)
www.barna.org

SAVE (Suicide Awareness Voices of Education)
8120 Penn Ave. S., Suite 470
Bloomington, MN 55431
952-946-7998
www.save.org
SPAN-USA (Suicide Prevention Advocacy Network)
1025 Vermont Ave., NW, Suite 1066
Washington, DC 20005
202-449-3600
www.spanusa.org

Yellow Ribbon Suicide Prevention Program
P. O. Box 644
Westminster, CO 80030-0644
303-429-3530
www.yellowribbon.org

Suicide Hotline
1-800-273-TALK (8255)

Canadian Mental Health Association: **www.cmha.ca**
Health Canada: **www.hc-sc.gr.ca**

Suicide Education and Information Centre:
www.suicideinfo.ca

Statistics Canada: **www.statcan.gc.ca**

World Health Organization: **www.who.int**

International Association of Suicide Prevention:
www.iasp.into